For
THOU
Art With Me

For
Thou
Art With Me

*Biblical Help for the Terminally
Ill and Those Who Love Them*

Bruce A. Baker, PhD

GRACE ACRES PRESS

CULTIVATING JOY

LARKSPUR, COLORADO

CULTIVATING JOY

Grace Acres Press
PO Box 22
Larkspur, CO 80118
www.GraceAcresPress.com

Printed in United States of America
25 24 23 22 21 20 19   01 02 03 04 05 06 07 08

Print ISBN: 978-1-60265-058-9
Ebook ISBN: 978-1-60265-059-6

Library of Congress Cataloging-in-Publication Data:

coming…

Table of Contents

1

Why Am I Writing This Book?

I am dying.

That statement, by itself, isn't all that remarkable, since it's true of all of us. Everyone reading these words is dying. What makes that statement unique is that my process of dying has been accelerated. After many visits and tests, and much poking and prodding, the doctors have told me that I have a terminal disease. In other words, I have an active illness that will inevitably end in my death. I won't die of old age. My disease will kill me.

In August of 2017, I was told that I have ALS. After trying on a few other diagnoses first, this is the only one that fit. When I asked about a prognosis, my neurologist said, "I'm fairly certain you will live six months. You could live a year, eighteen months at the outside." Since that time I've been told that the progress of my disease has been slower than expected. Now my doctors no longer guess at my life expectancy.

But my ultimate prognosis has not changed. At some undetermined time in the future, if everything remains as it is now, the muscles that control my lungs will stop working ... and I will die.

Drawing on my years as a pastor, I've discovered there are only two ways that a person may greet such news. The first is with varying degrees of fear. The second is with varying degrees of peace. I have never witnessed a third option.

At the extreme end of the fear spectrum is panic. I recently witnessed such panic in a person I met during one of my treatments. Bob (not his real name) is a likable enough fellow, but he is a driven man. Like me, he has ALS. He refuses to call his ALS "Lou Gehrig's disease" because it has nothing to do with Lou Gehrig. It is his disease. It is Bob's disease.

After his diagnosis, his sole mission in life was to find a treatment that worked. He told me that he couldn't go to the bathroom in the middle of the night without stopping by his computer and doing a search to see if some new breakthrough had been achieved. He ordered experimental medicines from India and Japan. He sent me videos on cannabis and nutrition that made extraordinary claims. Simply put, he refused to accept what the doctors told him. There must be — *MUST BE!* — something that worked.

When I asked him why he was afraid to die, he denied that he was. He said he was merely thinking of his wife and children and how to support them. But I knew he was lying. He never mentioned getting his finances in order or the plans he was making to provide for his family. His entire focus was on himself. On getting better. *On not dying.*

In contrast to Bob, there's ... well ... *me.* I'm not panicked. I'm not afraid. In fact, I'm routinely cheerful, and that makes me stick out (or at least so I'm told). Of the doctors and nurses that have attended me, the vast majority have commented on the extreme peace I exhibit — and most want to know why I have it. A few have asked me directly. More often they query my wife. One doctor asked my sister. But the majority opinion is that I am somehow different. That I'm not normal. That I am in possession of something the average individual does not have.

And that's why I'm writing this book. I want you to have what I have.

Really, there's nothing unusual about me. I'm just an average guy with a terminal disease. What makes me different is not who I am, but who I know and what he has promised. The good news is that you can know him too, and when you understand what that means—when you *really understand* what that means—you'll be like me: Just an average guy with a terminal disease who has a peace that surpasses all understanding.

Bruce A. Baker

November 20, 2018

Linger and Consider ...

Would you pause here for a bit and think about what we've discussed? These are important issues. Don't rush on to the next chapter without asking yourself these questions, and taking some time with your answers. Perhaps take time to discuss them with your spouse or a trusted friend.

Which word best describes my overall emotional state: *fear* or *peace*?

Would those who know me (family, friends, medical professionals, etc.) agree with my answer?

2

The Gift of Time

As I write this book, I'm making one grand assumption: namely, that you, the reader, have a terminal disease. Or, at least, that someone you love dearly has a terminal disease. Either way, your life has changed. It will never be the same. Now you're forced to think about death. You're forced to think about it every day.

Some people call this a curse. *I call it a gift.* It's a gift for two very important reasons: first, it leaves you no choice but to face the inevitable; and second, you've been given time to get ready. Now, obviously, all people, regardless of their health, have time to get ready. Everyone knows death is coming, and everyone should prepare for it. But really, who actually does that?

The wisest man who ever lived, King Solomon of Israel, once remarked that it is better to go to a funeral than a party. He didn't say going to a funeral was more fun — that obviously isn't the case — but going to a funeral is more necessary. It's necessary because *"death is the destiny of everyone; the living should take this to heart"* (Ecclesiastes 7:2). Put another way, it's easy to forget about death as we live our lives day-to-day. But all of us are going to die, and going to a funeral helps remind us of that.

The problem is, the corrective nature of a funeral is often short-lived. In our society, death has become something of an embarrassment. We don't like to think about it. We are afraid of it, so we try to forget about it as soon as possible. So, unless the departed is a close family member or friend, the helpful reminder that we're all going to die usually doesn't last long. Nevertheless, the ultimate statistic remains true: one out of every one person dies, and the wise person prepares for it.

Because this truth is so obvious, most of us would admit to it, at least in theory. The problem is that theory and practice seldom align as they should. Let me give you an example.

At the 1993 annual meeting of the American Heart Association, 30,000 doctors, nurses, and researchers met in Atlanta, Georgia, to discuss (among other things) the importance a low-fat diet plays in keeping our hearts healthy. Yet during mealtimes, they consumed fat-filled fast food — such as bacon cheeseburgers and fries — at about the same rate as people from other conventions. "'Food with a lot of fat in it just plain tastes good,' [Howard Gutgesell] said as he slurped his Wendy's Frosty, a chocolate ice cream dessert with 400 calories, 260 milligrams of sodium and 13 grams of fat, including 7 grams of saturated fat."[1] As I said, theory and practice seldom align as they should.

But now you have a terminal disease. Now you're *forced* to think about death. Now you have the time to make the preparations that you should've made all along.

This is a gift not everyone receives. Some people die suddenly, with no warning, no advance notice, *no time to get ready*. The routine trip home is ended when a drunk driver crosses the yellow line. A seemingly healthy man clutches at his chest, grimaces, and falls to the floor. In a random act of violence, a trigger is pulled and suddenly a family is bereft of a wife and mother. What these instances have in common (and scores of others just like them) is that *there was no time*.

There was no time to get finances in order.

There was no time to say goodbye.

There was no time to say those things that should've been said a long time ago.

There was no time to forgive.

There was no time to be forgiven.

Most importantly, *there was no time to get right with God!*

This isn't so with you. You have the benefit of a terminal disease. You know death is coming. You've been given the gift of time. You have time to do all those things that should've been done already.

Beloved, just like me, you've been given a gift. And, as is appropriate with all gifts, we should express our gratitude to the giver.

Thank you, O God, for giving me the gift of time.

Linger and Consider ...

At this chapter end, too, I'm going to ask you to stop ... rest ... think ... pause for a bit. There is nothing more important than your honest answers to these questions. Take the time. Give yourself, and those you care about, the gift of time spent thinking this through.

What is it I should be doing as I prepare for death?

Chapter 2

What words do I need to say to either forgive or be forgiven?

What is it I need to make right before I die?

3
Why Are People Afraid to Die?

In what is perhaps Sir Arthur Conan Doyle's most famous Sherlock Holmes story, "The Hound of the Baskervilles," Sir Charles Baskerville dies from a heart attack brought on by extreme psychological stress caused by an apparently supernatural dog. Although this makes interesting fiction, the main premise behind this story isn't all that far-fetched. Numerous scientific studies provide evidence of the possibility of being scared to death. In fact, one such study names this phenomenon "The *Hound of the Baskervilles* effect."[2]

In this study, researchers investigated whether cardiac-related deaths increased on the fourth day of the month among Chinese and Japanese people as compared to white Americans and Europeans. In Mandarin, Cantonese, and Japanese, the words "death" and "four" are pronounced almost identically; therefore, many Chinese and Japanese consider the number 4 to be unlucky. As a result, many Chinese and Japanese hospitals don't list a fourth floor or number any rooms "4" because they consider it jinxed. (Don't laugh. Many American hospitals don't have a 13th floor or room number "13" for the same reason.) Chinese and Japanese restaurants often avoid using the number 4. Some Japanese people avoid travel on the fourth day of the month, and the mainland Chinese omit the number in designating military aircraft.

What these researchers discovered is that, among this group, cardiac deaths were significantly higher on the fourth day of the month than any other day. In fact, the Chinese and Japanese population of California experienced a 27% higher mortality rate on this day than any other day. This effect was not evidenced in white Americans. So, what did the researchers conclude? "The Baskerville effect exists both in fact and in fiction and suggests that Conan Doyle was not only a great writer but a remarkably intuitive physician as well."[3]

The Baskerville effect may also be seen during the January 17, 1994, Northridge/Los Angeles earthquake. This was one of the worst earthquakes to strike the continental United States. It twisted highways and collapsed buildings. On the day of the quake, the coroner recorded five times more sudden cardiac deaths than would ordinarily be expected. More than 100 Californians literally died of fright, according to Robert Kloner, cardiologist at the Good Samaritan Hospital in Los Angeles. They didn't die because they were injured by falling debris or crushed under the rubble of collapsed buildings. No, they died because, when the earthquake hit, they thought they were about to die and that *thought* literally scared them to death.[4]

I don't think I need to do a lot of convincing that, in general, people's primary fear is the fear of death. Have you ever wondered why that is?

Human beings aren't afraid of death because it's uncommon. One hundred percent of people die. In all probability, someone you have known personally has died, whether it be a parent or grandparent or child or friend. Nearly everyone knows someone who has died. Therefore, we are on pretty firm ground when we say, "It's been done." Nor is our fear merely a case of beginner's nerves. People try new things all the time and most of those things don't produce any anxiety whatsoever. So, people's fear of death must come from another source.

The missionary anthropologist S. H. Kellogg lists four basic similarities among all religions, regardless of the nature of their belief systems.[5] In other words, all religions share four beliefs in common:

All religions assume the existence of a power or powers superior to humans, on which humans are dependent, and which is able to influence their destiny. People are born into this relationship and they are powerless to change it.

Because of each person's relationship to this supreme power or powers, people have certain obligations which must be met. Other actions must be avoided or suffering will result.

Between the individual and the supreme power or powers, something is wrong. Put another way, all religions appeal, in one way or another, to the individual person's sense of sin.

There is for each individual a state of being after death. The consequences of doing right or wrong in this present life follow a person after he or she dies.

Additionally, according to Kellogg, all people are naturally religious:

It is yet to be proved that any tribe has ever been found so degraded as to be utterly destitute of religious ideas. ... No doubt when we thus speak of religion as universal, we must use the word "religion" in a very broad sense; but however broad the sense in which we take it, it is still true that the possession of a religious faculty is one of the most distinctive characteristics of the human race.[6]

Of course, we don't need a missionary anthropologist to tell us this, for the Bible teaches the very same thing. In Romans 1:18–20, the apostle Paul argues that all people everywhere know and understand four facts about God:

The wrath of God is being revealed from heaven against all the godlessness and wickedness of people, who suppress the truth by their wickedness, since what may be known about God is plain to them, because God has made it plain to them. For since the creation of the world God's invisible qualities—his eternal power and divine nature—have been clearly seen, being understood from what has been made, so that people are without excuse.[7]

Please notice that, according to the apostle Paul, God is continually revealing *"his eternal power and divine nature"* through the created order. Put another way, people know that God exists (his ... divine nature), that he is personal (indicated by the personal pronoun "his"), and that he is eternal, and powerful. All people know this.

When we add this evidence together, the answer to why people fear death becomes obvious. All people know that 1) God exists, 2) that there is life after death, 3) that what one does in this life has a direct bearing on one's life after death, and 4) that between themselves and God something is wrong. ***This is why people fear death!*** They know that death isn't the end and that a real problem exists that determines what they will experience after they die. This is why people live their lives held in slavery by their fear of death (Hebrews 2:15).

Knowing why we are afraid to die does not help us overcome our fear of death. However, knowing the reason for our fear does help us find the antidote for our fear of death.

Linger and Consider ...

You know we're not done yet, don't you? Thinking about these things in the abstract may be difficult, but I'm going to ask you to go beyond the abstract. Take the time to sit quietly, and accept the discomfort as you consider how these ideas apply to yourself. It's important. Really, there's nothing more important, is there?

Answer this question honestly: Am I afraid of death?

If I wasn't allowed to use synonyms like nervous, anxious, apprehensive, and so forth, would my answer to the previous question change?

What do I know (or think I know) about what happens after I die?

4

How Can I Lose My Fear of Death?

Answering this question, above all others, requires the most accurate of information: if we get this question wrong, our eternity is at stake. Telling people what they want to hear simply will not do. Although this is especially true when speaking of eternity, it is equally true in all other areas of life as well.

The British ocean liner, the *R.M.S. Lusitania*, was struck by a torpedo from a German submarine on May 7, 1915. It appears that in an effort to minimize panic, the captain, William Thomas Turner, decided to shade the truth. Shortly after the torpedo struck the liner, one of the passengers, Charles Lauriat, returned to deck. Erik Larson tells what happened next.

> Lauriat was standing within earshot of the bridge when he heard a woman call out to Captain Turner, her voice steady and calm, "Captain, what do you wish us to do?"
>
> "Stay right where you are, Madam, she's all right."
>
> "Where do you get your information?" she asked.
>
> "From the engine room, Madam," he said. But the engine room clearly had told him no such thing. Apparently he was seeking to calm the crowd below and avoid setting off a panicked race for the boats.
>
> Lauriat and the woman now headed back toward the stern, and as they walked they told other passengers what the captain had said.

Second-class passenger Henry Needham may have encountered the pair, for he recalled that a passenger approaching from the direction of the bridge had shouted, "The Captain says the boat will not sink."

"The remark," Needham wrote, "was greeted with cheers & I noticed many people who had been endeavoring to get a place in the boats, turned away in apparent contentment."

Turner's words merely confirmed what the passengers and crew already believed, or wanted to believe: that no torpedo could cause the ship mortal damage. The ship's purser and surgeon spent the moments after the two explosions calmly strolling along the boat deck, smoking cigarettes, assuring passengers that the ship was not in any danger.[8]

The captain told them what they wanted to hear; he didn't want anyone to be upset. Thus, no one headed for the lifeboats. As a result, of the 1,959 passengers aboard the *Lusitania*, 1,198 perished. I think we can all agree that trying to make the people feel better by not telling them the truth was a disastrous strategy.

I mention this because telling the truth about eternity inevitably upsets some people. Many people are offended by the frank assessment concerning the condition of their souls that the Bible provides. I understand this—but I intend to press on anyway. For, you see, there is no way to remove the fear of death without dealing frankly with what the Bible says about God, about sin, and about the cross.

Definitions
First, we need to take care of a few definitions.

When I use the word *God*, I am referring to the personal,

triune God of the historic Christian faith as revealed in the Old and New Testaments. This God has revealed himself both in creation and in the Bible. This God is distinct from all other "gods" in all other religions. There is no way to blend or merge this concept of God with any other belief system. The only accurate portrayal of God is found in the Bible. If you can't accept that definition, you will probably find the rest of this book unhelpful. My entire argument rests upon the reality of this personal being and the truthfulness of his self-revelation in the Bible.

Another word that requires definition is the word sin. *Sin* is defined as any lack of conformity to the character of God. In other words, whenever we do something God wouldn't do, whenever we think something God wouldn't think, whenever we have an emotion that God wouldn't have, we sin. In the same way, whenever we fail to do something God would do, whenever we fail to think something God would think, whenever we fail to have an emotion God would have, we sin. Simply put, whenever we don't behave exactly as God would behave, we sin.

Finally, when I speak of Jesus, his death on the cross, and his resurrection from the dead, I am referring to real, actual historical events that occurred at a particular time and at a particular place. Some would call this story a myth. The Bible calls it history, so that's the way I treat it.

Now that we know what we're talking about, it's time to see what the Bible says about these subjects. For really, it is the intersection of these three topics that provide the remedy for our fear of death.

The Role of Sin
As we saw in the last chapter, people fear death because of their gnawing uncertainty about what happens after we

die. People know that between themselves and God, some-thing is wrong, and that this "something" determines their eternal destiny. The Bible calls this "something" sin.

The reason all people fear death is because all people have sinned. The apostle Paul makes this very clear:

> As it is written: "There is no one righteous, not even one; there is no one who understands; there is no one who seeks God. All have turned away, they have together become worthless; there is no one who does good, not even one." (Romans 3:10–12)

Now, I understand that this may sound a bit harsh. After all, we all know people who are, relatively speaking, good people. Perhaps you consider yourself a good person as well. Compared with other people you might rate at the high end of the scale. But that's not the point. The standard isn't other people. The standard is God.

According to the International Organization for Standard-ization (ISO), one cubic meter of air taken from an average room will contain more than 8 million particles that are 1 micrometer (μm) or larger. There will be more than 35 million particles that are half that size (0.5 μm). We would consider this a "clean" room. This isn't air taken from a woodworking shop, loading dock, or mechanic's garage. This is air taken from an office building or your living room.

However, this air really isn't really "clean," according to the ISO. In order to qualify as an ISO-1 clean room, there can be no particles suspended in one cubic meter of air that are 0.5 μm or larger.[9] None. Zero. Which means that if there is even one particle of that size in the room, the room isn't "clean." This might sound like an absurd standard for some, but it is necessary for the manufacture of certain pharma-ceuticals and semiconductors.

Well, it is the same way with us. We might consider ourselves clean, or at least as good as everyone else. But God's standard is different from ours. By God's standard, there can be no sin in our lives. None. Zero. Because God is completely, 100% holy, he cannot stand to even be in the presence of sin. Not even one sin. Therefore, the standard for dwelling with God is absolute perfection. We might say that heaven is the ultimate clean room, because there is no sin there. None whatsoever.

The Wages of Sin

One time a teacher of the law asked Jesus, *"Teacher, which is the greatest commandment in the Law?" Jesus replied, "Love the Lord your God with all your heart and with all your soul and with all your mind. This is the first and greatest commandment"* (Matthew 22:36–37). By making this the first and greatest commandment, Jesus shows us the magnitude of the problem. For who among us has ever kept this commandment? Have you? Has there ever been a time in your life where you loved God with every fiber of your being, with all that you own, with nothing held back, with no thought, no matter how slight, of self?

I didn't think so. For what it's worth, I never have either. Which means, of course, that if we were to number my sins they would have to be numbered by the moments of my existence, because this is a command that should always be kept and I have never kept it.

The Bible is also clear that my sin has earned a wage. That wage is death. Paul tells us, *"For the wages of sin is death..."* (Romans 6:23). A wage is something that is earned, and therefore, must be paid.

Suppose your employer said, "I want to let you know you've done a great job this week and I appreciate all your hard work. But I've got no paycheck for you today. It's not that I don't have the money, it's just that I've decided not to pay you." What would be your reaction? Undoubtedly you would argue that this is not an option. That money doesn't belong to him, it belongs to you. Why? Because you've earned it, that's why.

In the same way, our sin has earned a wage, and that wage must be paid. That wage is death. It is equally correct to think of the "wages" of sin as a debt that we owe. The wages of sin is death, but that death is something that we must pay. Because I have sinned, I owed a payment which consists of my life. Put another way, God must pay the wage of our death, which results in our owing the debt of our lives.

Therefore, because all have sinned, all die physically. That's fairly easy to see. But there is also a spiritual death, a second death that must be paid.

> *And I saw the dead, great and small, standing before the throne, and books were opened. Another book was opened, which is the book of life. The dead were judged according to what they had done as recorded in the books. The sea gave up the dead that were in it, and death and Hades gave up the dead that were in them, and each person was judged according to what they had done. Then death and Hades were thrown into the lake of fire. The lake of fire is the second death. Anyone whose name was not found written in the book of life was thrown into the lake of fire.* (Revelation 20:12–15)

According to this passage, anyone who is judged according to what they did in this life is thrown into the lake of fire. Why? Because the wages of sin is death, and everyone has sinned. The lake of fire is the second death. The only escape from this horrible fate is to have your name written in the book of life.

So, the question that must be asked at this point is this: "How do I get my name written in the book of life?"

Payment for Sin

It's important to remember that the wage for our sin must be paid. God is always just and therefore always pays what is owed. But please notice there is no requirement that the debt must be paid by us. Just as I could, if I chose, pay a bill that you owed with my money, so this debt maybe paid with someone else's death. And that's what happened at the cross.

Because Jesus had no sin of his own, he owed no debt—there was no need for him to die. There was no wage to be paid. As a result, he did not have to die, as we do, because he was not like us. Amazingly, though, he chose to die anyway. He said, *"No one takes [my life] from me, but I lay it down of my own accord. I have authority to lay it down and authority to take it up again"* (John 10:18).

Why would Jesus choose to die? Why would anyone choose to die?

Jesus said, *"Greater love has no one than this: to lay down one's life for one's friends"* (John 15:13). Jesus laid down his life because of his great love for us. He desires to dwell for eternity with us. He doesn't want us to go to hell. But he also knows that he has no other choice but to send us to hell, unless the problem of sin is taken out of the way. The wage must be paid. The debt must be collected.

When Jesus died on the cross, when he willingly gave up his life, he did so to pay our debt himself. He took on the sins of all people of all the world throughout all time, and he himself paid what we owe. Put another way, God took all the sin of all mankind and placed it on Jesus Christ.

We might say he took every sin ever committed and put it in Jesus' bank account. Then, instead of judging us, God judged Jesus for our sin. Jesus suffered the penalty: he paid our debt.

This means, in practical terms, that we no longer have to pay the penalty for our sins. Jesus did it for us.

Of course, this raises an obvious question. If Jesus paid the penalty for our sins, why is it so many people don't benefit from this? Why are people still cast into the lake of fire? Why do they still carry the burden of their sin?

On November 26 and December 6, 1829, two men, James Porter and George Wilson, robbed the United States mail, seriously wounding a mail carrier in the process. They were captured and brought to trial. On May 27, 1830, both defendants were sentenced to death. James Porter was executed on July 2, 1830. George Wilson, in contrast, received a presidential pardon from Andrew Jackson. In other words, he received a piece of paper that forgave his sins so that he didn't have to die. Amazingly, George Wilson turned down the pardon.

No one had ever done that before, so that the legality of such an action was uncertain. The case went all the way to the Supreme Court, which determined that Wilson was within his rights to turn down the pardon. Writing for the majority, Chief Justice Marshall delivered his opinion. As part of that opinion, he called a pardon "an act of grace" and laid down this principle:

> A pardon is a deed, to the validity of which, delivery is essential, and delivery is not complete, without acceptance. It may then be rejected by the person to whom it is tendered; and if it be rejected, we have discovered no power in a court to force it on him.[10]

The same may be said of the gift of forgiveness offered in Jesus Christ. Delivery of that gift is essential, and delivery is not complete without acceptance. We must actively accept the gift that Jesus offers. But how exactly does one do that?

The key word is "believe." Jesus said, *"Whoever believes in him [Jesus] is not condemned, but whoever does not believe stands condemned already because he has not believed in the name of God's one and only Son"* (John 3:18). To believe in him is to believe that he is who he said he was and that he did what he said he did. This means that you believe that Jesus really is both God and man, that he died to pay the penalty for your sins, and that he rose again to show that that payment was complete.

More than this, it means that you trust in this payment for your standing before God, and nothing else. It means that you're not trusting your good works, your baptismal certificate, the money that you give, your church attendance, or anything else that you **do** to earn your place before God. It means accepting the pardon that God offers and trusting in that and nothing else.

Chief Justice Marshall argued that a pardon needed to be formally presented in court. Until that was done, it had no value. In the same way, we need to formally accept the pardon that Jesus gives so that our names will be written in the book of life. So that our sins — all of them — will be forgiven; so that the issue of sin will no longer be between us and God.

So that we no longer need to fear death.

Linger and Consider ...

Please take a little while and think about these things. The next chapter won't disappear while you do. What we're considering here is the central question that affects your future. There may not be a lot of time left to you in this life, but there is time for this. Please rest here for as long as necessary to feel sure of your answers to these questions.

When push comes to shove, do I consider myself a sinner, or do I think of myself as a pretty good person, all things considered? (Hint: if you think of yourself as a pretty good person, you need to stop and reread this chapter.)

Have you ever accepted the pardon that Jesus offers? How do you know?

What are you trusting to be made right with God when you stand before him after you die? Is it his death and resurrection, or the good things that you have done in this life?

If you've accepted what Jesus did for you, how has this affected your feelings toward your own death? How might your feelings change based on your answers to these previous questions?

Are there family members or friends who need to hear about these things? Right now, as you face your own death, you may have the best of all possible platforms to share your faith.

5

Are There Answers as to Why Christians Suffer?

Late for a meeting, the businessman gets pulled over for speeding. As other cars whizz by, he rests his forehead on the steering wheel and whispers, "Why me?" The irreplaceable object crashes to earth at the feet of her two-year-old, and the busy mother covers her eyes with her hand and says, "Why this?" Dressed for her highly anticipated prom evening, the teen girl breaks a carefully manicured fingernail, and whimpers, "Why now?"

In these situations, the questions "Why Me?", "Why This?", and "Why Now?" are mere signs of exasperation—but they take on new significance when a doctor says you only have a limited time to live. That's when these questions deal (quite literally) with issues of life and death. You know what I mean. "Why would a loving God allow such a tragedy to overtake me?" "Why would God afflict me with the one disease I fear so much?" "Why would God take my life now, when I have so much to live for?" These are questions that require real answers, not just the hollow platitudes we read on inspirational posters.

If we are honest, we have to admit that life is hard, even in the best of times. When you have a terminal disease, sometimes ... well ... it's just *too* hard. Often others, even the ones who love us most, don't really understand how hard life can be. Whether it's the side effects of medications, the extra energy required for even the simplest of tasks, or the bone-weariness that comes from being so very tired all the time, these "complications" (what a terrible word) take their toll. So it's only natural that we ask the question "Why?"

Of course, we are not the only ones asking why. It is regularly true that it is more difficult to sit beside the bed than to be in the bed itself. To watch our loved one suffer is to suffer ourselves. Not only do the loved ones have to watch the objects of their affections suffer such hardship, but they also have to deal with the utter helplessness of their own situations. They would take away the pain if they could, but they can't. They would give the loved ones their strength and their sleep if they could, but they can't. *They would trade places if they could, but they can't.*

Not only this, but our caregivers face an additional set of problems, problems that didn't exist before "the diagnosis." After all, the groceries still have to be bought, the laundry done, the grass cut, the bills paid. Life goes on even when we wish it would stop just long enough for us to catch our breath. But now, added to the common stresses of everyday life are mounting medical bills, insurance problems, daily medications, and the constant difficulty of not having enough time to do it all. It's understandable, therefore, when our caregivers whisper the question: "Why?"

The problem of suffering, in general, is a vexing one for every thinking person. In fact, it is the so-called "problem of evil" that is a major objection to Christianity by those who do not believe or obey the gospel. For a believer, though, suffering presents a special set of problems. After all, it's easy to point to a fallen world to explain why dogs have fleas and why people get sick. The world has been corrupted by sin, and sin brings heartache.

That, of course, is true as far as it goes. But when you're Christian, that answer doesn't completely make sense, because we claim God the Almighty, the creator and sustainer of all that is or was or will be, as our Father. He is the one who describes himself as gracious and compassionate, slow to anger and abounding in lovingkindness, whose mercies never fail, whose compassions are new every morning, and whose faithfulness is from everlasting to everlasting. He is the one who pities those who fear him as a father pities the son he loves.

Knowing this to be true, why is it that Christians suffer? Why doesn't God just smooth out the way for us instead of letting such heartaches come? An even better question is: Why does God actively bring such trouble into our lives? Ecclesiastes 7:14 tells us that God has made both the day of prosperity and the day of adversity. Knowing this to be true, why doesn't God just make good days? Why do the bad days have to come?

In answering these questions, we must start with the understanding that God is not random. Everything he does, he does for a purpose. Therefore, part of trusting him is believing that there is a good and proper purpose underlying or behind all our suffering. After all, if God really is all-powerful, and if he really does only what is good, then we have to believe that all his decisions are decisions that we ourselves would make if only we knew everything he knows and were as good as he is. His decisions, therefore, are ones that we will not only approve of, but also rejoice in when we get to eternity.

Knowing this to be true, it is certainly within bounds to investigate the reasons for suffering as described in the

Bible. Therefore, the next three chapters address these three questions: Why me? Why this? Why now?

Linger and Consider ...

Would you pause here for a bit and think about what we've discussed? These are important issues. Don't rush on to the next chapter without asking yourself these questions, and taking some time with your answers. Perhaps take time to discuss them with your spouse or a trusted friend.

Why me? Why this? Why now? Have I asked myself (perhaps secretly) any — or all—of these questions?

Do I feel guilty about asking these questions? What answers did I come up with? How confident am I that these answers are correct?

6

Why Me?

God in his goodness has provided several specific answers to the question "Why do Christians suffer?" Some of these answers aren't directly applicable to the problem of terminal illness (e.g., persecution from an unbelieving world, see 2 Timothy 3:12–13; John 15:18–21), so they aren't discussed here. Others, however, are directly applicable and are discussed in this book. Not all of these reasons will apply to your specific situation, but at least one will, and most likely more than one.

Sometimes We Suffer as Part of the Call of God

Before I was afflicted I went astray, but now I obey your word. (Psalm 119:67)

Many times the call of God at the very beginning of our Christian life involves suffering and affliction. This is easy to see, isn't it?

In Acts 16, the Philippian jailer, in fear for his life because he thought the prisoners had escaped, was about to kill himself when Paul shouted out, "We are all here," and then led him to Christ. In John 4, a "nobleman, whose son was sick," was terrified that his son might die, so the man came to Jesus and trusted in him. There was the woman with the bleeding disease in Luke 8 who came to Christ as a result of her illness. In Matthew 15, there was a woman of Canaan whose daughter was demon-possessed who came to Jesus because of her fear for her daughter. This list goes on and on.

I have no doubt that many reading these words could testify that it was trouble and trial that God used to break their will and bring them to the Savior. That work continues even today. It could be that your illness is designed for your ultimate good: that is, that you may trust in Jesus Christ and his finished work on the cross and his resurrection from the dead so that you might be saved. If this is the case, though this physical suffering is troublesome, the eternal benefit you will receive from it is so far beyond the cost as to not be compared.

Sometimes We Suffer as the Consequences of Our Actions

Do not be deceived: God cannot be mocked. A man reaps what he sows. Whoever sows to please their flesh, from the flesh will reap destruction; whoever sows to please the Spirit, from the Spirit will reap eternal life. (Galatians 6:7–8)

To understand these verses in their original context, we must recognize that Paul is speaking to believers. It is to members of the church that he gives this instruction.

Please notice that Paul begins with a warning: *"Do not be deceived."* This shows that it is all too easy to be deceived in this area. It shows that all of us are vulnerable to the notion that our actions don't have consequences. Paul tells us not to be deceived into believing this lie.

He then moves on to the laws of sowing and reaping. The laws of sowing and reaping are these: (1) You harvest what you plant, (2) You harvest more than you plant, and (3) The harvest is certain, even if it is delayed. For example, if I plant beans in a field, I may wander up and down the side rows praying diligently for a good corn crop, but when it comes time to harvest, I'm going to get beans. Not only am I going to get beans, but I'm going to get way more beans than I planted. Finally, even though there is a time delay between when I planted and when I harvest, the harvest will eventually come. At some point in the future, sooner or later, I'm going to harvest beans. In the same way, the laws of sowing and reaping apply to our lives as well.

At this point I want to stress that this has nothing to do with our forgiveness before God. Our forgiveness before God is totally and solely dependent upon our belief in Jesus Christ and what Jesus did on the cross. The things that we do or don't do are immaterial to the question of our salvation.

That being said, whether you are a believer or an unbeliever, the laws of sowing and reaping apply to you. The reason they apply to you is because of their purpose. God has instituted these laws so that he will not be mocked. If we sow to the flesh, from the flesh we will reap destruction.

In practical terms, what does this mean? Well, if I get drunk, steal a car, get in an accident, and lose a leg, I can most certainly confess my sin before God and be forgiven and restored to fellowship. This is undoubtedly true. But it is also true that my leg won't grow back and most likely I'm going to jail. In the same way, if I've smoked a pack a day for the past 40 years, I shouldn't be surprised if I now have chronic obstructive pulmonary disease (COPD). It's all a matter of sowing and reaping.

Now, although all this is true, we must quickly add that in Joel, God says that he can restore or repay the years that the locusts have eaten (Joel 2:25). In other words, God can give back wasted years. He can graciously remake a life ravaged by sin, and he often does. But it also remains true that much of the suffering in our lives is the result of our own sinfulness, if we will just admit it.

We should also realize that *this reason never exists alone.* God is working all things together for the good of those that love him (Romans 8:28). If you allow him to, God will use this time of trial to bring about righteousness in your life and encouragement to his people.

Sometimes We Suffer Because of God's Discipline of Sin

Endure hardship as discipline; God is treating you as his children. For what children are not disciplined by their father? If you are not disciplined — and everyone undergoes discipline — then you are not legitimate, not true sons and daughters at all. Moreover, we have all had human fathers who disciplined us and we respected them for it. How much more should we submit to the Father of spirits and live! They disciplined us for a little while as they thought best; but God disciplines us for our good, in order that we may share in his holiness. No discipline seems pleasant at the time, but painful. Later on, however, it produces a harvest of righteousness and peace for those who have been trained by it. (Hebrews 12:7–11)

Have you ever noticed that when someone gushes, "Oh, I just love children," they really don't mean that? What they mean is that they love *well-behaved* children. I have never met anyone who enjoys the society of undisciplined, spoiled children. You know the type of children I mean. I'm speaking of those children whose sinful nature has not been restrained, and as a result are textbook examples of self-centeredness, arrogance, and disobedience. I think we can all agree that children need discipline.

I understand that nearly everyone reading these words is no longer a child. The days of parental discipline are long since past. Nevertheless, as much as we hate to admit it, we all need to be disciplined from time to time by our Heavenly Father. Please understand that I'm not talking about being punished for sin. All that punishment was poured out at the cross. Jesus took it all. Instead, I'm speaking of the discipline that is within the family, the kind of discipline that brings about holiness.

Such discipline shouldn't be considered unusual or only for the especially sinful. Even well-behaved children still need the discipline of their parents. If they don't receive it, they won't stay well-behaved for long. So it is with us. Hebrews 12:8 states that everyone undergoes discipline. In fact, if we are never disciplined by the Lord, the text tells us that we are illegitimate children and not true sons/daughters at all.

This certainly makes sense when you think about it. As a rule, we don't discipline other people's children (although there are exceptions). We only discipline our own children. Parental discipline is an indication that we are in the family. In fact, it is a sign of the love of God that he disciplines us. Jesus said in Revelation 3:19, *"Those whom I love I rebuke and discipline."* Put another way, the motivation for our discipline is not anger, it is not spite, there is no lingering malice involved. No, it's those who are loved by God who are rebuked and disciplined.

I admit this might sound odd at first blush, but when you take a moment and consider the implications, it makes perfect sense. When you're a child, you're envious of the kid on the block who's ignored by his parents. He comes and goes as he pleases and wherever he pleases. He never has to be home at a certain time. If he skips school, no one seems to care. To the immature, this seems to be an enviable situation. But is it really?

It is the child who is loved that has the curfew. It is the child who is loved that has the boundaries. It is the child who is loved that has the rules enforced. Put another way, it is the child who is disciplined that is the child who is loved.

The text of Hebrews argues that because we didn't hate our earthly fathers for disciplining us as children, we shouldn't turn bitter against our Heavenly Father when he does the same thing. Even though the spankings we receive are painful for a moment, they produce a harvest of righteousness and peace for those who have been trained and corrected by them.

Knowing this to be true, the author of Hebrews encourages us to strengthen our feeble arms and weak knees. We are not to become permanently disabled spiritually by this discipline, but rather strengthened and healed by it (Hebrews 12:13).

Sometimes We Suffer So That Christian Character May Be Produced in Us

Consider it pure joy, my brothers and sisters, whenever you face trials of many kinds, because you know that the testing of your faith produces perseverance. Let perseverance finish its work so that you may be mature and complete, not lacking anything.
(James 1:2–4)

In this passage we read about how the testing of our faith ultimately brings about Christian maturity. Suffering, it seems, unlike anything else, develops in the believer perseverance, or what we might call stick-to-it-iveness. It teaches us not to give up, but rather to rely on God in a moment-by-moment dependence, which is what God desires from us at all times anyway.

There are two biblical illustrations of what this process of producing Christian character is like. The first is that of a refining fire and the second is that of a plant. Let's look at each in turn.

The apostle Peter writes:

In all this you greatly rejoice, though now for a little while you may have had to suffer grief in all kinds of trials. These have come so that the proven genuineness of your faith — of greater worth than gold, which perishes even though refined by fire — may result in praise, glory and honor when Jesus Christ is revealed. (1 Peter 1:6–7)

The picture here is of gold being placed under intense heat. As the gold melts and turns to liquid, all the imperfections either float to the surface so that they may be skimmed off or are burned away by the fire. What is left is the purest of gold, without the defects and flaws it previously had.

The second illustration comes from the words of Jesus. In John 15:1–5 we read,

I am the true vine, and my Father is the gardener. He cuts off every branch in me that bears no fruit, while every branch that does bear fruit he prunes so that it will be even more fruitful. You are already clean because of the word I have spoken to you. Remain in me, as I also remain in you. No branch can bear fruit by itself; it must remain in the vine. Neither can you bear fruit unless you remain in me. I am the vine; you are the branches. If you remain in me and I in you, you will bear much fruit; apart from me you can do nothing.

Those of us who have ever had gardens understand the truth of this teaching. No gardener ever just allows the plant to grow without tending it. There is a pruning process in which those growths that take away from the fruitfulness of the plant are removed. This process is never haphazard, nor is there any cruelty on behalf of the gardener. In fact, every good gardener cherishes the plants and desires their growth. Good gardeners take delight in going to the garden and assessing the growth of the stalk, in gauging the size of the fruit, or even in bragging to their friends about the fruitfulness of the plant.

This reflects, at least in some way, the delight of the father as he watches us mature, as he sees the fruit, as he gently guides us to ever more fruitfulness. Those acts of pruning must come, but they are never instances of vindictiveness or carelessness. No, they are acts of love for our own good.

Sometimes We Suffer So That We Might Comfort Others

Praise be to the God and Father of our Lord Jesus Christ, the Father of compassion and the God of all comfort, who comforts us in all our troubles, so that we can comfort those in any trouble with the comfort we ourselves receive from God. For just as we share abundantly in the sufferings of Christ, so also our comfort abounds through Christ. If we are distressed, it is for your comfort and salvation; if we are comforted, it is for your comfort, which produces in you patient endurance of the same sufferings we suffer.
(2 Corinthians 1:3–6)

As believers, we don't merely experience our own suffering: we also enter into the sufferings of others in the body of Christ. We rejoice with those who rejoice and weep with those who weep. As I look back at my years in the pastorate,

I cannot count the number of times when I've been moved to tears as I spoke with another member of the body. And I know this experience is not unique to me. You know what I'm talking about, don't you?

When we see another believer in distress, it's only natural that we want to comfort them. It doesn't matter to us why that one is suffering. A true believer desires to comfort another in the body. This being said, although we share the same Spirit and possess the same Bible, the best comfort comes from the one who has suffered in the same way as the one suffering.

I don't know how you're suffering today, but I do know that this trial, which is certainly unique in its details to you alone, is nevertheless common to all mankind. You aren't the first to suffer in this way, and you certainly won't be the last. But because God cares for his people so much, he often allows us to suffer some special trial in order that, further down the road, we may be a comfort to others who are hurting as we are.

At this point I should be quick to add that this isn't a one-to-one proposition. You don't suffer to help just one other individual. No, the comfort that we receive — and we do receive comfort from the Savior, don't we? — will later bless the hearts of many other believers as we share in their burdens and comfort them with the same comfort we've received.

Sometimes We Suffer Because of Conflict in the Spiritual Realms
One day the angels came to present themselves before the LORD, and Satan also came with them. The LORD said to Satan, "Where have you come from?"
Satan answered the LORD, "From roaming throughout the earth, going back and forth on it."

> *Then the* Lord *said to Satan, "Have you considered my servant Job? There is no one on earth like him; he is blameless and upright, a man who fears God and shuns evil."*
>
> *"Does Job fear God for nothing?" Satan replied. "Have you not put a hedge around him and his household and everything he has? You have blessed the work of his hands, so that his flocks and herds are spread throughout the land. But now stretch out your hand and strike everything he has, and he will surely curse you to your face."*
>
> *The* Lord *said to Satan, "Very well, then, everything he has is in your power, but on the man himself do not lay a finger." Then Satan went out from the presence of the Lord. (Job 1:6–12)*

There are several important lessons for us to learn from this text.

First, notice that the reason for Job's suffering was none of the reasons we've mentioned so far. Instead, Job was put on display to teach the angelic realm about the faith of a believer.

Second, we should observe that Job's suffering was always under control. Satan complains that God put a hedge around Job and everything that he has. He says in essence, "I can't touch him until you allow me to." When he takes up Satan's challenge, God says that everything Job has is Satan's but that Satan is not permitted to touch Job himself. There is a limit to how much suffering God would allow in Job's life.

Satan comes back in chapter 2, when God once again brags on Job. After repeating his initial assessment of Job, God says, *"And he still maintains his integrity, though you incited me against him to ruin him without any reason"*

(Job 2:3). Again, please notice that there was no physical reason for Job's suffering. There was nothing you could point to in Job's life that could account for the trial he was going through.

Satan isn't finished. He counters that a man will give everything he owns for his life. "But if you let me touch him ... I haven't been able to do that yet, you stopped me, but let me touch him ... that's all it will take." So God moves his protection back one more step. He allows Satan to touch Job physically, but refuses to allow Satan to take his life. As a result, Job is afflicted physically in every way imaginable.

What is important to notice is that Job, when it is all finished, never finds out why these things happened. As we read through the book, we know, but Job never did. Still, it is important to see that there was a reason. It was a reason that didn't cut short God's love for his servant. It was a reason that has resulted in Job's being honored from that time till now.

What was true for Job may be true for you. Perhaps God has said, "Have you considered my servant <u>insert your name here</u>, that there is none like him/her on the earth; that he/she is blameless and upright, someone who fears God and shuns evil?" It could be that you are teaching the angelic realm something they would never learn otherwise. And like Job, it may be that you will never find out the reason for your suffering.

The Benefit of This Study
Knowing that there is a reason for our suffering helps us ward off the nagging suspicion that somehow God is unjust or that he is capricious and unfeeling, with no sympathy for the suffering of his people. Nothing could be further from the truth. God has some good purpose for the suffering you're experiencing now.

Linger and Consider ...

Here we are again, at the end of another chapter, and you know I'm going to ask you to stop for a bit. Don't hurry past this opportunity.

Of the reasons we discussed (listed below), how might they apply to me? Don't spare yourself the pain of self-examination. Be honest — ruthlessly honest — as you answer this question.

Sometimes we suffer as part of the call of God.

Sometimes we suffer as the consequences of our actions.

Sometimes we suffer because of God's discipline of sin.

Sometimes we suffer so that Christian character may be produced in us.

Sometimes we suffer so that we might comfort others.

Sometimes we suffer because of conflict in the spiritual realms.

How does understanding that there is a reason for my current suffering change my attitude toward life in general and God in particular?

What comfort from God am I receiving in the midst of my suffering? Is there any way that I might comfort others with the comfort I have received from God?

7

Why This?

Understanding that there is a reason for suffering may answer the question "Why me?," but there are other questions that must be answered. For example, some at this point might be saying, "Yes, well, it's all well and good to give reasons why believers in general may suffer. But that only helps so much. It doesn't answer the question as to why my particular suffering had to take this form. Why did *this* have to happen?"

This question is generally asked by people in two specific situations. There may be other reasons why people ask this question, of course, but generally speaking it is one of two particular circumstances that prompt this question.

First, this question arises when someone's individual trial is something they have feared for a long time. For example, suppose someone has witnessed the debilitating effects of a stroke upon a parent or other loved one. Witnessing that physical and mental crippling in the past has made an indelible mark. I know someone of whom this is true. I have heard them say, "I'll take cancer, but I never, ever want a stroke." But now, through the providence of God, what they have feared most has happened. The most natural question therefore becomes: *"Why this?"*

Second, "Why this?" is asked when the pain, regardless of whether it is physical or emotional, is so severe that the patient is stretched almost to the breaking point. In this case, it is not the fact of the suffering but the intensity of the suffering that becomes the most burning question.

In attempting to answer questions concerning the specifics of your own personal suffering, the most truthful answer is also (at least at first blush) the most unhelpful: "I don't know." I can't say with certainty anything about the unique situation in which you find yourself. There are simply too many variables. In fact, even if I knew all that could be humanly known concerning the facts of your case, my answer would still be the same: "I don't know." I don't know because, simply put, God has not revealed the mysteries of his will in this matter.

That being said, while "I don't know" is not the most satisfying answer, it appears to be the most righteous answer. We looked at the beginning of the book of Job in the last chapter. Now we need to examine the ending.

In the midst of Job's intense suffering, three of his friends show up to "comfort" him — but their "comfort" is of no help whatsoever. They make God into someone who is fully predictable, almost mechanistic, in his actions toward humanity. If you do what's right, you will be blessed. If you do what's wrong, trouble will come your way. But we all know that's not correct. Sometimes the wicked prosper and sometimes the righteous suffer … and all of this is in accordance with the will of God. That's why, at the end of the book, God condemns these three friends by saying, *"[These three] have not spoken of me what is right, as my servant Job has"* (Job 42:8).

Well, if these three friends spoke what was wrong and Job spoke what was right, the obvious question is this: What did Job say that was right? We need to know this so that we may speak correctly, just as Job did. The answer is found in the last chapter of the book.

Throughout the book, Job continually stresses his innocence and questions God's justice with regard to his suffering. He longs to take God to court and question him face-to-face to learn why all this has happened. God does not allow himself to be questioned, but cross-examines Job instead.

God describes examples from the created order and repeatedly asks Job if he has either the wisdom or the strength to accomplish such things. This has a profound impact upon Job. He at once confesses his ignorance and declares God's greatness.

> *Then Job replied to the LORD:*
>
> *"I know that you can do all things; no purpose of yours can be thwarted. You asked, 'Who is this that obscures my plans without knowledge?' Surely I spoke of things I did not understand, things too wonderful for me to know.*
>
> *"You said, 'Listen now, and I will speak; I will question you, and you shall answer me.' My ears had heard of you but now my eyes have seen you. Therefore I despise myself and repent in dust and ashes."* (Job 42:1–6)

It's important to note that God praises Job for speaking the truth about him. Specifically, Job acknowledges God's sovereign wisdom and confesses his own arrogant ignorance. Put another way, Job says this: "God, you're right and I'm wrong. When I challenged your goodness or your faithfulness or your justice I was merely showing my ignorance. Now that I understand who you really are, I repent of my sin."

Thus, at the end of the day, it comes down to this: we are called to have an abiding trust in who God is, knowing that his ways are best. "I don't know" is the only appropriate answer regarding why God does what he does. That being said, in the midst of our ignorance concerning the mystery of God's will, we should be willing to say with Job: *"Though he slay me, yet will I hope in him"* (Job 13:15).

Linger and Consider ...

"Why this?" That is almost certainly one of the questions that has brought us together in these pages. Please give yourself time to think about it before you proceed to the next chapter.

Have you ever considered "I don't know" to be a righteous answer?

Have you questioned God's goodness, or his faithfulness, or his compassion during this time of testing?

Even though all these questions seem to go unanswered, are you willing to accept the testimony of the Bible, and say with Job, *"My ears had heard of you but now my eyes have seen you. Therefore I despise myself and repent in dust and ashes?"*

When all is said and done, are you willing to say with Job, *"Though he slay me, yet will I hope in him?"* Answer truthfully. Don't lie about your struggles. It doesn't do anyone any good.

8

Why Now?

⁓After our previous discussion, I hope you are convinced that there is a reason for your current suffering. You might not know why this suffering has taken the form that it has, but I hope you have determined to continue trusting in the goodness and faithfulness of God, even when you don't have all the answers. But there is one more question with regard to suffering that should be answered: "Why now?"

Why is God ending my life now, just when business is picking up, or just when we're putting our marriage back together, or just after the death of my [father, mother, grandparent, in-law, aunt, uncle, son, daughter, best friend, etc.], or any of dozens of other possible reasons? Why now, when everything is going so well? Or, why now, when we have so much trouble as it is?

These are legitimate questions, to which I must again plead ignorance. As before, I'm unable to provide specifics for each individual case. But just as the Bible provides a list of possible explanations for the reason behind your suffering, so the Bible gives insight into the possible basis for the timing of your suffering.

The prophet Isaiah writes:

> *The righteous perish, and no one takes it to heart; the devout are taken away, and no one understands that the righteous are taken away to be spared from evil. Those who walk uprightly enter into peace; they find rest as they lie in death.* (Isaiah 57:1–2)

This is something we often don't consider. God knows all things that may be known. He not only knows those things that have been, are, and will be, but he also knows the infinite possibilities of all that might've been or could be. Which means that he knows what our futures hold. He knows both the evils that we will face and the evils we will cause. He even knows those evils that will come about through our lives indirectly.

A prime example of this is the case of Hezekiah. In 2 Kings 20:1–11 we read the story of Hezekiah's illness. He is at the point of death when the prophet Isaiah comes to him with a word from the LORD: *"Put your house in order, because you are going to die; you will not recover"* (2 Kings 20:1). No reason is given for this pronouncement; it is simply given as a statement of fact. This is what God has determined, so put your affairs in order.

Hezekiah was a good king who walked faithfully before the LORD with wholehearted devotion. He did what was right in God's sight, and he reminded God of this in a prayer in which he wept bitterly. In response to this prayer, God promised to add fifteen years to his life. Undoubtedly everyone who loved Hezekiah saw this as good news. But, with the benefit of hindsight, we realize it wasn't as good as it appeared.

During those fifteen extra years of life, Hezekiah fathered a son, Manasseh. Unlike his father, Manasseh was an evil king. In fact, he led Judah into so much sin that God said he would hand Judah over to her foes. He would wipe out Jerusalem as one wipes out a dish, turning it upside down. It was the sin that Manasseh brought upon Judah that was the final straw for God. It was his sin that was the ultimate cause of Jerusalem's destruction.

Now, to be clear, we don't know what would've happened to Judah if Manasseh had never been born. But we do know what *did* happen to Jerusalem because Manasseh was born. This evil was brought upon Jerusalem because Hezekiah lived those extra fifteen years.

But that's not all.

During those fifteen extra years of life, Hezekiah received an ambassador from the faraway city of Babylon. During that visit Hezekiah showed the ambassador everything that was in his storehouses. He showed him the silver, the gold, the spices, and the fine oil. He showed him the armory and everything that was found among his treasures. He held nothing back. Everything in his palace and in all his kingdom Hezekiah showed to the ambassador and his entourage.

After this ambassador's visit the prophet Isaiah once again comes to see Hezekiah. When he learns that Hezekiah showed his visitors all his wealth and treasure, Isaiah foretells the outcome of such a foolish move. Because of this, everything that has been stored up to this day will be carried off to Babylon. Nothing will be left. Even some of your own descendants will become eunuchs in the palace of the king of Babylon (2 Kings 20:12–18).

Now again, we don't know what would've happened if Hezekiah had not shown all his wealth to the ambassadors from Babylon. But we do know what happened because he *did* show his wealth to the ambassadors from Babylon. Once again, evil was brought upon Jerusalem because Hezekiah lived an extra fifteen years.

When God bring something into our lives, and we would change it, we would only make things worse. Perhaps the reason this trouble has been brought upon you now is because God knows the evil that will come into your life that could be avoided by your death. Or God knows the evil that will come to others because of those extra years. Either way, the timing of this trouble is not random or haphazard. God, who knows all things that will be or even might be, has picked the very best time.

The Ultimate Answer Is Faith

These last few chapters have addressed three questions that are common to those with terminal illness: Why me? Why this? Why now? Ultimately, the answer to each of these three questions comes down to faith. Oh, of course the Bible has provided possible answers for some of these questions, but absolute certainty is something that God has withheld from us. It is evidently his will that we trust in him regardless of our current circumstances. So, regarding these three questions, as in all things, it is best to say with Job: *"Though he slay me, yet will I hope in him"* (Job 13:15).

Linger and Consider ...

Let's stop again and think about this chapter, and its implications. These aren't new questions we face. All throughout the Scriptures, we read of people wrestling with these things. Again, we ask you to set aside time and approach this in an unhurried fashion.

List things you know about God's character that will be a help when you struggle with questions about your illness. Choose some Scripture passages to post prominently to remind yourself. Consider choosing some passages to commit to memory, so you can meditate on them in difficult times.

9

What Is Death for a Believer?

Although the next statement may be rather obvious to some, I will make it anyway: *What happens after death is not the same for everyone.* In fact, death for a believer is so radically different from death for an unbeliever that the difference prompts us to do a thorough examination.

Without question, anguish about death is the reason for most of the suffering in this world. Whether it is because of a fear of impending death or the grief endured because of the loss of another, death is unquestionably an evil. The Bible teaches that death is the consequence of sin. Death brings separation and sorrow. The Bible portrays death as an enemy that has invaded the land of the living. Even the Lord Jesus did not look forward to his own death, despite his confidence that he would be raised from the grave. As I said, death is an evil.

Nevertheless, the Bible helps us accept the tragedy of death by teaching us what we would never have expected to hear: that God can make death a good and gracious gift. After all, as the apostle Paul says, *"And we know that in all things God works for the good of those who love him, who have been called according to his purpose"* (Romans 8:28). Please notice that God is working "in all things" for the good of those who love him. Not "some things," or "most things," or even "nearly all things." No, God is actively working for our good "in *all* things." This includes those things that are unquestionably evil, like death.

Understanding that God can (and does) work even evil things, such as death, together for our good, it seems appropriate to ask, "What is death for a believer?" I believe there are (at least) four biblical descriptions of death that we need to consider.[11]

It Is a Key in a Door

When I saw him, I fell at his feet as though dead. Then he placed his right hand on me and said: "Do not be afraid. I am the First and the Last. I am the Living One; I was dead, and now look, I am alive for ever and ever! And I hold the keys of death and Hades.
(Revelation 1:17–18)

Immediately prior to this passage, the apostle John hears a voice behind him and turns to see who's speaking. What he sees is terrifying in the extreme: He sees a vision of the risen Christ, but not as Christ was on earth. His hair is white and his eyes are like blazing fire. His feet are like glowing bronze and his voice is like the sound of rushing waters. He is dressed in a robe reaching down to his feet with a golden sash around his chest.

On seeing this vision of Christ, John passes out from fear. In all fairness, who wouldn't? The bravest soul I find in the Bible is Daniel, who, on experiencing a similar vision of Christ, drops to his hands and knees, starts shaking violently, and begins to hyperventilate. In all honesty, if this were to happen to me, almost certainly I would follow John's example and faint.

This being said, I love the first words out of Jesus' mouth. He says, *"Do not be afraid."* Jesus and John always shared special love for one another. It was a love beautifully expressed at the Last Supper, when John leaned against

Jesus' breast. Now here, once again, you can almost hear the tenderness in Jesus' voice as he says, "Don't be afraid."

Then he says, *"I am the First and the Last. I am the Living One; I was dead, and now look, I am alive for ever and ever! And I hold the keys of death and Hades."* All of these words are designed to bring comfort to John, just as the vision initially brought terror. And when you consider the context, this makes perfect sense.

For, you see, in this passage the emphasis is upon the death and resurrection of Jesus Christ. *"I am the First and the Last"* points to his eternity. *"I was dead"* is better translated, "I became dead." In other words, against all expectations, and in direct contrast to his being alive from eternity past and living on into eternity future, the Eternal One entered the state of death. Yet he didn't stay dead. Now he is alive for ever and ever, never to die again. He will never die again because his death on the cross accomplished all that was necessary to bridge the gap between the Holy God and the believing sinner. Because of this death and resurrection, Jesus states that he holds the keys to death and Hades (the place of the unbelieving dead).

The implications of this statement are staggering. The fact that Jesus holds the key to death means that no one dies unless he puts the key in the door. In practical terms, this means that no army, no matter how great, can kill me unless Christ puts the key in the door. In the same way, no team of doctors, no matter how skilled, can save me if he does.

Beloved, this is a great comfort when you understand who God is. The standard way to describe the character of God is that he is gracious and compassionate, slow to anger and abounding in lovingkindness. Which means, of course, that he waits until the absolute best time, having weighed the alternatives, to put the key in the door. So we can be assured that if we had the ability to go back and undo that tragic accident, undo the illness, undo the death, we would only make things worse. Jesus knows the right time to put the key in the door.

This also shows that your diagnosis is no mere chance occurrence. There really is no such thing for a believer. God knows the best time. Whatever the circumstances that he brings about, they are best for you and for your family and for your friends.

It Is a Change in Location

Therefore we are always confident and know that as long as we are at home in the body we are away from the Lord. For we live by faith, not by sight. We are confident, I say, and would prefer to be away from the body and at home with the Lord. (2 Corinthians 5:6-8)

When a believer dies, the body is laid to rest, but the real person — the real you — experiences a change in location.

If death were all that there is, if it really was the end, it would be more than appropriate for the dying and their loved ones to mourn without ceasing, because there would be no way that they would ever see one another again. But death isn't the end. To be away from the body is to be at home with the Lord.

What does this mean *exactly*? For most of us, the best we could do in answering this question would be to utter some vague generalities that we've picked up along the way. But the Bible gives us more help than that. When the apostle Peter speaks of our future inheritance, he uses four word pictures to describe it.

Praise be to the God and Father of our Lord Jesus Christ! In his great mercy he has given us new birth into a living hope through the resurrection of Jesus Christ from the dead, and into an inheritance that can never perish, spoil or fade. This inheritance is kept in heaven for you.... (1 Peter 1:3–4)

The first word, "imperishable" (NIV "never perish"), means that our inheritance is not corruptible, that it will not pass away. It will not rot or decay. All decay is a change from better to worse. But the paradise of God is like God himself: without change and without end.

Our inheritance is also "unstained" or "undefiled" (NIV "can never ... spoil"). The idea is that it is untainted by evil. So again, we see that God's paradise is just like God himself: completely untouched by sin.

This world has been ravaged by sin and is therefore wracked by death and misery. Even at the best of times, sin is always present to mar the beauty of God's creation. The consequences of sin are always with us here, but sin has no place there, in God's paradise. Our inheritance there is completely unspoiled by the devastation of sin.

The apostle Peter also tells us that our inheritance is "unfading" (NIV "can never ... fade"). In the original language, this word was used of flowers and suggests a supernatural beauty that doesn't grow old with time. Put another way, it is forever pleasing and new, always fresh and entertaining, without the slightest hint of ever becoming commonplace or routine.

When we put these three words together, we see that our inheritance is untouched by corruption or decay, unstained by evil, and unimpaired by time. It is composed of immortality, purity, and beauty. It is a wondrous place unlike anything we've ever experienced.

Finally, we see that this inheritance is "kept," or "reserved," for us. The original language emphasizes a state that already exists. In other words, this inheritance is a present reality which God himself guards for us to ensure that we receive what he has promised — and this is an important part of our hope. The enemies of the gospel might destroy all that we have in this world. They may ruin our reputations and drive away all our friends. But there is no force in all of creation that can even touch our inheritance, because it is being reserved for us by God himself.

When a believer dies, he changes location. He moves from this present world, which is filled with decay, ravaged by sin, and fading away with the passing years, to the inheritance of God which is like God himself: incorruptible, undefiled, and untouched by time. It exists even now and God is guarding it for us.

It Is an Answer to Prayer

"Father, I want those you have given me to be with me where I am, and to see my glory, the glory you have given me because you loved me before the creation of the world." (John 17:24)

Whenever a believer is terminally ill, it normally follows that the believer is praying during his time of testing. Usually, other people are praying for him as well. These prayers may take a number of forms, but usually they include some petition for healing. What we often fail to realize, however, is that Jesus has prayed for each and every believer, and that his prayer seems to be directly contrary to the ones we make at such times.

Jesus' prayer is that we might be where he is: that is, heaven. He desires that we be there with him so that we may see his glory. The importance of this request cannot be overstated, for it is the last petition in his last prayer immediately prior to his agony in the garden and his crucifixion. Put another way, the last thing Jesus asks — the last thing he desires — is that we might be with him where he is.

Now, the obvious question at this point is why would Jesus make such a request? After all, doesn't he realize the suffering that death brings? Doesn't he care about the pain and apprehension of the one that is dying? Is he oblivious to the grief suffered by those left behind? Is he really so uncaring that he is unconcerned with the heartache of his people? Or is he just blissfully ignorant of what it really means to be human? Does he really love us, or is it all just a charade?

A careful reading of this prayer dispels these thoughts. It shows us not only that Jesus loves us, but also the extent of his love.

Jesus had already prayed, *"And now, Father, glorify me in your presence with the glory I had with you before the world began"* (John 17:5). Very soon Jesus would take his place at the right hand of God the Father, in the midst of all the angels and archangels and the entire company of heaven crying out praise to both the Father and the Son. But the prayer recorded in John 17:24 makes it very clear that Jesus would not be satisfied with that state of affairs. What he wanted, what he earnestly prayed for, was that all those who would believe in him (John 17:20) would be there with him, enjoying the glories of heaven with him, experiencing his happiness with him.

For, you see, when he prayed thus, Jesus was about to die for us. He left the glories of heaven, became a man, and suffered the worst death imaginable, so that we might be with him. In fact, we are a gift to Jesus from God the Father. When he prays to the Father, he calls us *"those you have given me."* And so Jesus prays that his gift might be delivered. Jesus' final prayer indicates his great love for us. He's not willing to do without us.

Now, we need to think carefully about what this does, and does not, mean. It does not mean that Jesus needs us in order to be happy. This simply isn't the case. As God, he has no needs. God, because he is who he is, is completely self-sufficient. There is nothing outside of himself that he requires either for his existence or for his complete happiness. Thus, whenever we say, "God needs ..." we are wrong by definition. God has no needs.

That being said, while it is true that God has no needs, it does not follow that God has no desires. There are numerous examples of this in Scripture. For example, God doesn't want *"anyone to perish, but everyone to come to repentance"* (2 Peter 3:9). This desire does not stem from any personal lack that God is experiencing; rather, it comes from his great love for us. He would not be harmed in the slightest if everyone perished. But because he loves us, he doesn't want to see that happen.

Well, it is the same thing here. Because of his great love for us—remember, this prayer was given immediately prior to his dying for us—Jesus prays that we would be with him to see his glory because that is the best of all possible circumstances we could experience.

Because this is so difficult for us to realize, it seems wise at this point to review the testimony of one who's been there. The apostle Paul speaks of a man who was caught up to heaven (2 Corinthians 12:2). By the way he writes this account, most biblical scholars believe that he is referring to his own personal experience. He states that he *"was caught up to paradise and heard inexpressible things, things that no one is permitted to tell."* That being said, he is able to give a brief description of where he went, calling it *"paradise"* (2 Corinthians 12:4). Although Paul does not elaborate any further on this experience, it is clear that it changed his outlook on death forever.

When faced with an uncertain future, when death was a real possibility, Paul stated that he was torn in his desires. He acknowledged that his staying alive was important to his readers. The opportunity for fruitful labor remained open to him. They would benefit from his future ministry. Therefore, it was necessary for him to *"remain in the body"* (Philippians 1:24). That being said, to depart and be with Christ was *"better by far"* (Philippians 1:23). In fact, to die was gain (Philippians 1:21), because to depart meant he would *"be with Christ"* (Philippians 1:23).

It's important for us to see why Paul would say dying was gain. It's not for the reasons we typically think.

When Paul wrote these words, he was in prison (Philippians 1:14, 17). Even before he was imprisoned, he had some sort of physical ailment described as a *"thorn in my flesh, a messenger of Satan, to torment me"* (2 Corinthians 2:7). One of his friends, the apostle James (Galatians 1:18–19), had already died because of his testimony for Christ (Acts 12:2). Paul too had already suffered much for his testimony for Jesus. He had received five brutal floggings. He had been beaten with rods three times. He had been stoned once and left for dead. He had been shipwrecked three times. He was in constant danger as he moved from place to place and often went without proper food and clothing

(2 Corinthians 11:24–28). Clearly, his life was not one of comfort and ease. His life was one of pain, danger, and immense stress.

Knowing this to be true, it's not so difficult to see why he might have longed for death. His suffering would be over. He would be reunited with his lost loved ones. His pain would be gone. Everything that makes this life not worth living would be done away with. But, interestingly, he lists none of these reasons as to why he might choose death over life.

The reason he desires to *"depart"* is that he would *"be with Christ, which is better by far"* (Philippians 1:23). In other words, it wasn't the elimination of suffering that he longed for. It was being with Jesus that he craved. Remember, he knew — first-hand — what this was like. That experience was burned into his memory, and it changed his entire outlook on life and death.

The only other individual who can provide first-person testimony as to what this is like is Jesus himself. Jesus is the only one who can testify to exactly what Paul experienced. Jesus alone can bear witness to the glory that awaits us after death: and that glory is so amazing, so incomprehensible, so beyond what words can express, that Jesus prays for the best evidence of all. He prays that we might experience it.

He wants us to see that from which the angels hide their faces (Isaiah 6:2). He wants us to experience the glory that is the light of the eternal city (Revelation 21:23). He desires that we have resurrected bodies so that we will have an immediate view of his person (Job 19:26–27). Put another way, he wants us to experience an eternal state that is the best of all possible worlds, namely, that we would be with him where he is and see his glory.

So he prays to that end.

Thus it happens, in the life of every believer (until Jesus returns) that God the Father says "no" to our prayers and says "yes" to the prayer of his Son. God says "yes" because of his great love for the Son and because of his great love for us.

It Is the Delivery of the Gift

For it is by grace you have been saved, through faith— and this not from yourselves, it is the gift of God—not by works, so that no one can boast. (Ephesians 2:8–9)

Jesus loves us so much that he prayed we would be with him one day so that we might behold his glory. It is a glory far greater and more wonderful than anything this world can produce. As we saw in the section before this, this prayer is asking for the delivery of a gift. Jesus is praying for *"those you have given me."*

In a very real sense, though, the delivery of this gift to Jesus is also the delivery of a gift to us. Paul tells us our salvation is a "gift of God." It's true that we experience our salvation in a limited sense now. But it's equally true that our salvation will not be complete until we reach eternity. Only then will we be completely free from the ravages of sin and its companion, death.

Understanding our salvation in its fullness means that we must recognize that this is not our true or final life. There is something much greater and much more significant than the life we now live in the flesh. There is something beyond the present that is infinitely more important that what is in the here and now; there really is no comparison.

The present life can be compared to a training ground for eternity. It is the mere entrance, like a porch on a great mansion. It's like the preface of a book that contains many chapters. Although the porch of that mansion might be beautiful, it is vastly inferior to the wonders that lie inside. The preface of a book gives us some clue as to the author's purpose, but it is not the most important feature. Both the porch and the preface are insignificant in comparison to that to which they lead.[12] In the same way, our life now is so vastly inferior to the life that is to come that we may rightly say: when believers die, they are receiving a gift that was purchased for them long ago.

"Better by Far"

At the beginning of this chapter, I stated an obvious truth: death is an enemy. Nothing I have said has changed that. But God, who works "all things" for the good of those that love him, takes from this evil something wonderful.

All people die—but not all deaths are the same. Death, for a believer, is different. It's a key in a door, it's a change in location, it's an answer to prayer, and it's the delivery of a gift. When we really believe all this, we can say, with Paul, that to depart and be with Christ is "better by far."

Linger and Consider ...

Our culture works very, very hard to avoid thinking about death. But perhaps now is the time. No ... actually, I'd say now is surely the time. Will you set aside a few minutes to think about this?

How does knowing that death is a key placed in a door by Jesus himself affect my view of the timing of my diagnosis and the progress of my disease?

How does understanding that my death involves a change in location and is the answer to Jesus' prayer provide me comfort? Does this provide me with more peace and contentment than I had previously?

If I really believe that to depart and be with Christ is "better by far," how should this affect my general attitude toward life? What changes should I make in my life's orientation to reflect this belief?

10

What Is It Like to Die?

In my years as a pastor I've heard many people say, "I'm not afraid of death, but I am afraid of dying." At first blush, this may sound like a distinction without a difference, but actually it isn't. It is a legitimate concern. When people make this statement, what they are really saying is this: "I am comfortable and secure when I think of my eternity. But the process of getting there gives me pause."

I don't know, but I strongly suspect that the reason for this unease is that we know almost nothing about the process. Let's be honest: fear of the unknown is common to nearly everyone. That being said, "almost" nothing is not "absolutely" nothing. The Bible does provide a few details that should give us comfort.

First, and perhaps most importantly, we know that the LORD is with us throughout the entire process. In perhaps the most famous Psalm in the Psalter, David sings, *"Even though I walk through the valley of the shadow of death, I will fear no evil, for you are with me; your rod and your staff, they comfort me"* (Psalms 23:4).[13] In this context the *"valley of the shadow of death"* is not actually death itself, but rather the threat of death. As we have already seen, death, throughout the Bible, is considered an evil. But even when death is threatening, David will fear *"no evil."* Put another way, whether it is the threat of death or death itself, David sings that he will not be afraid. No matter what form the evil may take, David refuses to be afraid. He will fear *"no evil."*

The reason David will not be afraid is what is important. In this song he claims no special strength or courage. There are no abilities of his own that provide him confidence. No, he may be fearless in the face of death for one reason and one reason only: "you are with me." In other words, just as the LORD had been with him in life, so he will be with David in death. Throughout the process already known to untold millions, yet still unknown to us, the LORD will walk with us through the valley of the shadow of death. We won't go through it alone. Like the loving father that he is, he will hold our hand and be with us and guide us through this transition.

Second, we know that the process of death is different for believers and unbelievers. Please note that carefully. It's not just that the results of death are different for believers and unbelievers: the process of death itself is different. We know this because Jesus has given us a case study involving the death of a believer and an unbeliever.

In Luke 16:19–31 we read the story of the rich man and Lazarus. Some people consider this to be a parable, but I don't believe this to be so. Parables are always anonymous. *"A farmer went out to sow his seed"* (Matthew 13:3), or *"the kingdom of heaven is like a man who sowed good seed in his field. But while everyone was sleeping, his enemy came and sowed weeds among the wheat"* (Matthew 13:24–25), or *"the kingdom of heaven is like yeast that a woman took and mixed into a large amount of flour"* (Matthew 13:33). Do you see the pattern? There is a farmer, a man sowing good seed, an enemy, a woman — common individuals without names. But here that pattern is broken. Although the identity of the wicked man is unknown, the righteous man is singled out by name: Lazarus.

In this story, Jesus is giving his first-person testimony concerning an event that actually happened. This isn't just an interesting tale, this is history. Because this is the record and recollection of an actual event, we may infer that the details listed here are common to the process of death. We may also identify those things that are different for believers and unbelievers.

In both cases it appears that death is instantaneous. When the rich man opens his eyes, he is already in a place of torment (Luke 16:23). The apostle Paul states that those who are away from the body are at home with the LORD (2 Corinthians 5:8). Thus, it appears that there is no prolonged journey, no tunnel with white lights, no transition stage when death occurs. In one very real sense, death is closing our eyes in this world and opening them in the next.

The difference between these two deaths is that the angels carry Lazarus to paradise, while there is no mention of ministering spirits with regard to the rich man. In other words, it appears that all the resources of heaven are employed for the well-being of the righteous at the time of their death.

As far as I know, the Bible has nothing else to say regarding the process of death itself. Nevertheless, though not all of our questions have been answered, we've been given enough information to provide the comfort that we need. The LORD is with us throughout the entire process. We close our eyes in this world and open them in the next without any arduous intermediate process. God sends his angels to carry us directly to himself.

Knowing all these things to be true, it is not only possible, but it is also right and proper to sing with David, *"Even though I walk through the valley of the shadow of death, I will fear no evil, **for you are with me.**"*

Linger and Consider …

Would you pause for a while and think about this chapter? Don't rush past. Wait here with an open heart, and think about these things.

I'm comforted by the fact that the angels carry us to the presence of God. Does this thought provide you comfort as well?

The fact that the LORD is with us through the process of death is designed to take away fear. What is it — exactly — about the LORD being with us and death that provides us the courage we need to "fear no evil?"

11

What About the Resurection of the Body?
or Hope For Those Left Behind

*Brothers and sisters, we do not want you to be unin-
formed about those who sleep in death, so that you do
not grieve like the rest of mankind, who have no hope.
For we believe that Jesus died and rose again, and so
we believe that God will bring with Jesus those who
have fallen asleep in him. According to the Lord's word,
we tell you that we who are still alive, who are left until
the coming of the Lord, will certainly not precede those
who have fallen asleep. For the Lord himself will come
down from heaven, with a loud command, with the
voice of the archangel and with the trumpet call of God,
and the dead in Christ will rise first. After that, we who
are still alive and are left will be caught up together
with them in the clouds to meet the Lord in the air. And
so we will be with the Lord forever. Therefore encourage one another with these words.*
(1 Thessalonians 4:13–18)

The stated purpose of this book is to provide biblical help
for the terminally ill. But, as we all know, the terminally
ill patient is not the only one who struggles during this
time of crisis. We who love the one who is sick wrestle with
the diagnosis as well. Watching the inevitable decline of
our loved ones is a trial like no other. Contemplating life
without our loved one causes many of us to teeter on the
brink of despair.

Grief is an emotion unlike any other. When we grieve, we
think that we will never smile again. We are amazed that

the sun still shines. We wonder that people can still talk and joke on the streets and that the world goes on just as it had before, while ours has crumbled to bits. Does the Bible offer any comfort for the one who shudders and sobs at the sight of a vacant chair?

God, being ever the loving father, understands our grief. After all, *"he knows how we are formed, he remembers that we are dust"* (Psalm 103:14). Therefore, it should be no surprise to learn that there is a passage of Scripture written specifically to console us in our affliction.[14]

In 1 Thessalonians 4:13–18, the apostle Paul writes of those who have died *"in Christ."* Thus, this passage clearly addresses the future agenda for Christians who have died. Paul's description of Christ's coming for his church (the *"dead in Christ,"* as well as *"we who are still alive"*) was written so that his readers would not *"grieve like the rest of men, who have no hope"* (1 Thessalonians 4:13).

It's important to notice that Paul's stated intent is not that people would not grieve. Grieving is natural. Jesus himself had first-hand knowledge of the agonies of grief (John 11:33–36). Still, there are certain truths that, when properly understood, make the grieving process less intense. These truths are examined in this passage. In fact, we are commanded to take what Paul has written and *"encourage each other with these words"* (1 Thessalonians 4:18).

What this means in practical terms is that, while comfort can be found here for everyone contemplating their own death, in this context, this comfort is specifically directed at those who are grieving. The assurance of Christ's return, the resurrection of the dead, the change that occurs in those who are still alive, and our forever being with the Lord is directed specifically to those whose loved one has been taken by death. These promises are given to those who can no longer sing in church, for those whose tears flood their lonely beds. They are for those bent low by sorrow, beaten down by heartache, hollowed out by grief. Paul says to those weeping beside an open grave *"encourage each other with these words."*

The Basis for Our Hope

In this passage, when Paul speaks of Jesus' return for his church and the resurrection of the body, he grounds his message on two historical events. Put another way, Paul's teaching here should be believed because of what Jesus did and what he said. Let me show you what I mean.

The central tenet of the Christian faith is Jesus Christ's death and resurrection. If you do not believe this, then you aren't a Christian. It's really as simple as that. This is why Paul begins his argument by saying, *"we believe that Jesus died and rose again."* He wants to make sure the reader knows that the foundation of what he is about to teach lies at the core of Christianity. In other words, if you accept the central tenets of biblical Christianity, then you must accept what is being taught here.

The teaching that Jesus is coming again is a doctrine that has been mocked by this world for a long time. You don't have to pay too much attention to confirm that statement. Still, the reason so many people refuse to take the coming of our Lord Jesus seriously is that they don't take the cross seriously. Pulpits that don't speak of the cross and the empty tomb can hardly be expected to preach his coming again.

However, if we believe that Jesus came the first time, that he took our sins and paid for them on the cross, and hold fast to the testimony of Scripture that Jesus rose from the grave three days later, then it's not much of a leap to expect him to return and conquer the grave again.

So, the first basis for belief in the coming of our Lord Jesus is his death and resurrection. The second basis is found in verse 15. We read that this teaching is *according to the Lord's own word."*

Now, we don't know exactly what "word" of Jesus Paul is referring to, because he isn't specific in this statement. It's likely that Paul is thinking of the words Jesus spoke in the upper room on the night before his crucifixion. On that night Jesus said to his disciples,

> *My Father's house has many rooms; if that were not so, would I have told you that I am going there to prepare a place for you? And if I go and prepare a place for you, I will come back and take you to be with me that you also may be where I am.* (John 14:2–3)

In other words, Jesus said he is coming back to get the disciples. "I'm going to take you to be with me," Jesus said.

It could be that Paul is remembering the great prayer Jesus prayed for his disciples and for those who would believe their testimony, as recorded in John 17:24. Jesus prayed, *"Father, I want those you have given me to be with me where I am, and to see my glory, the glory you have given me because you loved me before the creation of the world."* It's also possible that Paul personally received some special revelation from the risen Lord, although I think this is somewhat unlikely given the plain statements of Jesus we've just read.

Still, it doesn't really matter what statements of Jesus Paul has in mind. The basis of Jesus' coming again for his church is the credibility of Jesus himself. It's according to the word of the Lord, Paul says. So, if you believe in the death and resurrection of Jesus and if you believe he is a credible witness regarding the future, then you should have no trouble believing what follows.

One Event in Four Steps
Even though Paul is describing one great event, he breaks it down into four specific steps. First, Jesus comes down (verse 16). Second, he shouts a command (verse 16). Third, the dead come forth (verse 16). Fourth, we are caught up (verse 17). So, let's look at each step in turn.

First, Jesus comes down. Now, the obvious question is: from where? To answer that question, we must know where Jesus is now. Verse 16 tells us that Jesus comes down "from heaven." Paul tells us, in Romans 8:34, *"Christ Jesus, who died—more than that, who was raised to life—is at the right hand of God and is also interceding for us."* So we see that Christ leaves the presence of God in heaven and descends to earth for this event.

In 1 Thessalonians 4:16, Paul states that *"the Lord himself"* will come down from heaven. Though this isn't as clear in our English translations, a special emphasis is placed upon the pronoun in the original language. Thus, we might translate it like this: *"none other than the Lord himself comes down."* Put another way, Paul is saying this event is too important to be left to a surrogate. This isn't a job for a messenger or a deputy. No, when Christ comes for his Bride, he will do so himself, even if it means leaving the glories of heaven for a second time.

Second, Jesus shouts a command. The word translated as *"command"* is a military word. It's used, for example, in the Greek translation of Proverbs 13:27, where the locusts march at one word of command. We see an example of this when, at the tomb of Lazarus, Jesus shouts, *"Lazarus come out"* (John 11:43).

Paul uses this military term, I believe, to illustrate the absolute sovereignty of Jesus in this matter. In other words, there is nothing optional about what is going to happen. This is completely in accordance with the Lord's will and nothing can hold it back. When Jesus lets loose a shout of command, there is no question about whether or not he will be obeyed. The event described here is certain.

Third, the dead come out. It's clear that the dead actually take precedence in this event. Certainly, it is a blessing to be alive when this happens, but if we are not, we won't miss it. The dead rise first.

Now, if the event described here follows the same pattern as the rest of Scripture, the graves will burst open when this happens. You'll remember that the Lord Jesus ordered Lazarus' tomb opened before he was raised from the dead. Likewise, Jesus had the stone rolled away prior to his resurrection. So I believe there will be open graves, serving as a telltale sign for all the world that the dead in Christ have risen and that death has been defeated.

When this happens, the entire church will stand on earth together, united for the first time. At that one glorious moment it won't matter what denomination you belonged to, how you were baptized, your race, your country, or anything else that divides the church today. The only thing that will matter is if you are "in Christ."

Finally, according to verse 17, we are caught up. The verb translated as *"caught up"* denotes a sudden and forcible seizure, an irresistible act of snatching away. This verb is used in Acts 23:10, where we read, *"The dispute became* *so violent that the commander was afraid Paul would be torn to pieces by them. He ordered the troops to go down and **take him away from them by force** and bring him into the barracks.*"

So we see that this *"catching away"* is not merely hit or miss. It is the result of Christ's mighty command and is executed with irresistible force. As a result, the saints have no options in this matter. This is one area where there is no opportunity for disobedience. In the same way, there is nothing on earth that can prevent this from taking place. Nothing in all of creation can stop the Bridegroom from claiming his Bride. It is an event that no one and nothing can hinder.

The Benefits of This Resurrection
The first thing we should notice is that those who have died in Christ are said to be *"sleeping"* in verse 13. We should be quick to add that this isn't the sleep of the soul. Paul writes in 2 Corinthians 5:8 that to be away from the body is to be present with the Lord, so the sleep here refers to the sleeping body only. This makes perfect sense when you consider that verse 14 states that Jesus is bringing with him those who have fallen asleep. Therefore, at this event, there will be a reuniting of the soul with the body.

This picture of sleeping is a common way for the New Testament to describe the death of a believer. Lazarus was said to have fallen asleep when he died (John 11:12-14). The bodies of many saints who were raised from the dead after the resurrection of Jesus were said to have *"fallen asleep"* in Matthew 27:52. The godly deacon Stephen *"fell asleep"* when he was stoned to death in Acts 7:60. At the church of Corinth, Paul announced the judgment of death upon many because of the careless way that they approached the Lord's table. It was said of them that a *"number sleep"* (1 Corinthians 11:30).

What is really comforting about the statement is the expectation that comes with sleep. When someone has fallen asleep, the expectation is that they will wake up again. In fact, our English word *cemetery* comes from the Greek word meaning "sleeping place." Which means, of course, that when we place a believer in the grave, it isn't as permanent as it seems at the time. It's temporary. It's only for a season. The sleeping believer will wake up again.

Throughout my many years as a pastor, I've officiated at a lot of funerals. Whenever I do an interment for a believer, and I stand beside that open grave, I like to tell those assembled, "This is where the miracle takes place. One of these days, and no one knows when, this grave will burst open and our loved one will no longer sleep!"

Second, please notice that a great reunion is going to take place. Verse 17 tells us that we will be caught up together "with them" who have fallen asleep, so we will all be with the Lord forever.

Let's be very honest with one another. The hardest part about death is the separation that occurs. Sometimes the last words are less than kind. Sometimes the suddenness of the departure leaves no time for making amends. But the reality of a bodily resurrection, after which we will be with the Lord forever, gives an abiding comfort that the separation is only temporary.

Finally, there is the comfort of an eternal blessing in verse 17. There's no better way to describe what it means to be forever with the Lord than with the words of the apostle John in Revelation 21:3–5:

And I heard a loud voice from the throne saying, "Look! God's dwelling place is now among the people, and he will dwell with them. They will be his people, and God himself will be with them and be their God. 'He will wipe every tear from their eyes. There will be no more death' or mourning or crying or pain, for the old order of things has passed away." He who was seated on the throne said, "I am making everything new!" Then he said, "Write this down, for these words are trustworthy and true."

Because we shall forever be with the Lord, we should obey the command given in verse 18. We should be encouraging one another with these words.

A Practical Application

Before we leave this passage of Scripture, we should notice that no signs are given for this event. There is nothing to look for, nothing to be fulfilled. This is an event that could take place at any moment—and that fact should have an impact on the way we live, shouldn't it?

The story is told of a little girl who, after church, where she had been taught about the coming of Jesus, started quizzing her mother.

"Mommy, do you believe Jesus will come back?"

"Yes."

"Could he come this week?"

"Yes."

"Today?"

"Yes."

"Could he come in the next hour?"

"Yes."

"In a few minutes?"

"Yes, dear."

"Mommy, ...would you comb my hair?"

That's the kind of attitude we should have at all times. Jesus could return in a few minutes, so we should keep our hair combed.

I don't know about you, but I've started listening for the shout. For it could be today.

Linger and Consider ...

We ask again ... one more time: Would you pause here for a bit and think about what we've discussed? These are important issues. Don't tuck this book away without thinking through what's just been discussed. Do some writing about these questions, and perhaps review your thoughts on previous chapters.

This passage of Scripture is written specifically to provide comfort for those who grieve the loss of a loved one. Be sure you share this chapter with those who love you. Consider whether leaving behind something in writing, or a video, that references this chapter might be an encouragement.

Your disease is crippling your body in any number of possible ways. Understanding that God still has a plan for your body — that it will be resurrected and made new — how does this affect the way you look at your illness?

The return of Jesus could happen at any time, even today. Should this fact affect the way you live right now? Why or why not?

12

What About Assisted Suicide?

Note: For this discussion I am making a distinction between the termination of life and the termination of treatment. This distinction, and its implications, are discussed in the final few paragraphs of this chapter.

Inevitably, when I teach about the glories that await the believer after death, I'm asked the question, "Well, if things are as wonderful as you say, why not just commit suicide and get there quicker?" Some people ask this sarcastically. The implication is that things can't be that wonderful, or at least you can't really believe that it's that wonderful, or you'd end your life right now. For others there is a real urgency behind this inquiry. For those with a terminal illness, the logic is relatively straightforward: I'm going to die anyway. Life is so difficult right now. Something so much better awaits. Why shouldn't I die at the time, and by the method, of my own choosing?[15]

More often than not, in our contemporary society, this question is framed around the idea of human rights. The unstated assumption is that my life and my body belong to me. Therefore, I should be able to dispose of each as I choose. But to frame the question as a human rights issue is actually to ask the wrong question. We should not be asking, "What are my rights?", for this question places humans at the center of the issue. The better question is, "What does God say?" If God really exists, if he really is our creator and judge, if he really is the absolute standard by which we judge all moral questions, then his opinion (and not our own) is what is most important.

That's why, when it comes to the topic of medically assisted suicide, it's that vital we understand the pronouncements of God. For suicide does not end it all. If you believe the Bible, then you must believe that your conscious existence continues after the death of your body. In fact, the immaterial part of you — that part of you that makes you "you"— not only continues to exist, but also is able to remember the events of this life (Luke 16:25). Not only will the events of this life be remembered by you, but they will also be remembered (and reviewed) by God. It's true that there is a separate judgment for believers and unbelievers with separate emphases and differing results. But the activities of this life (including suicide, medically assisted or not) will be inspected by the judge of all the earth. Therefore, it is of utmost important that we know the mind of God on this issue.

What Does God Say About Suicide?

The most relevant passage for discussing suicide, medically assisted or otherwise, is found in the Sixth Commandment: *"You shall not murder"* (Exodus 20:13; Deuteronomy 5:17).

Now, I recognize that the minute I bring up the Ten Commandments, some people bristle. We live in a society that thrives on exceptions and special circumstances. As each person's situation is unique, so then what is right and wrong must adapt to each individual's state of affairs. We don't like absolute rules that allow no wiggle room. Which is why so many of us don't like the Ten Commandments.

The Ten Commandments are presented in the Bible as absolute, without qualifications, without conditions. They are presented as abstract and eternal principles which transcend all circumstances. As Thomas Cahill, in his *New York Times* bestseller *The Gifts of the Jews*, puts it:

[The Ten Commandments] require no justification, nor can they be argued away. They are not dependent upon circumstances, nor may they be set aside because of special considerations. They are not propositions for debate. They are not suggestions. They are not even (as a recent book would have us imagine in the jargon of our day) "ten challenges." They are exactly what they seem to be — and there is no getting around them or (to be more spatially precise) out from under them. ... They have been received by billions as reasonable, necessary, even unalterable because they are written on human hearts and always have been. They were always there in the inner core of the human person — in the deep silence that each of us carries within. They needed only to be spoken aloud.[16]

Because of this, the Ten Commandments can be somewhat difficult to hear. Yet, because they are what they are, if we are to know the mind of God, we must deal with them. More specifically, for our discussion here, we must understand what is meant by the Sixth Commandment: *"You shall not murder."*

First of all, I suppose, we should understand what is, and is not, covered by this command. Of all the words used for "killing" in the Old Testament, the word used here is the closest word to our English word *murder*. This Hebrew word can be used to describe murder (premeditated killing) or manslaughter (accidental killing). But because manslaughter is dealt with separately (and differently) in Deuteronomy 19:1-13, it seems clear that this commandment does not include accidental killing. By the same principle, this commandment does not apply to defending one's home from nighttime burglars (Exodus 22:2), execution of murderers by the state (Genesis 9:6), or involvement in war (Numbers 31:7). As this word is used only for the killing of human beings, this commandment does not include animals.

Second, we should notice this commandment has no direct object. It doesn't say, "you shall not murder someone else," or "you shall not murder your fellow human beings." No, it simply says, *"you shall not murder."* From this we must conclude that the commandment not only forbids the murdering of someone else, but also the murder of one's own person, or suicide. This really shouldn't be all that surprising. If God considers human life to be sacred and worth protecting (and he does), it seems a stretch to say that this commandment protects the life of every human being except you.

Third, we should recognize that behind this specific commandment lies a greater and more general principle. According to the apostle Paul:

> *The commandments, "You shall not commit adultery," "You shall not murder," "You shall not steal," "You shall not covet," and whatever other command there may be, are summed up in this one command: "Love your neighbor as yourself."* (Romans 13:9)

If we were to put that another way, we might say it like this: The commandment *"do not murder"* is merely an elaboration on the more general command to *"love your neighbor as yourself."* Therefore, we should view this prohibition on murder not only through the lens of what is forbidden, but also through the lens of the good that it encourages. This commandment should be regarded as a consequence of our higher duty to preserve life whenever possible. Even when the taking of another human life is permitted (Exodus 22:2) or even commanded (Genesis 9:6), there remains the idea of the preservation of life in the larger community. And if this commandment encourages the good of preserving life generally, it follows that it encourages the preservation of your life specifically.

Now, at this point someone is undoubtedly saying, "But you don't understand. My life is not good. My life is one of pain, and suffering, and humiliation. What is 'good' is not the preservation of my life but the ending of it."

Although this argument has a strong emotional appeal, and I have sympathy for it, it betrays a common misconception about what it is that makes a life "good." "Good" is not the same as "pleasant" or "desirable." What makes a life "good" is actually independent of our experience.

We must remember that when God created the human race, he made them, male and female, in his own image (Genesis 1:26) and he personally breathed into us the breath of life (Genesis 2:7). In other words, the reason we have life is because God has given it to us. Additionally, every single human being manifests the image of God. This image is completely independent of a person's abilities, talents, intelligence, or usefulness. Every single person bears the image of God because they are human beings and because God has given them life. Because humans are created in the image of God, any attack upon any human being is an attack on God by proxy (Genesis 9:6).

Perhaps this last point requires clarification, as it might not be immediately clear. When I was in the Navy, our ship was scheduled to pull into a Turkish port. Before we were given liberty (free time ashore), we were warned about how to behave. We were told the case of a sailor on a previous ship who drank too much and thought it would be funny to relieve himself on a statue of Atatürk, the founder and first president of the Republic of Turkey. Unlike the inebriated sailor, the government of Turkey *did not* find this funny. They arrested him and placed him in prison, where he sat while his ship pulled off and left him. The reason they took such a harsh line against this unfortunate young man was because the people of Turkey considered an attack upon the image of Atatürk an attack upon Atatürk himself.

Well, it is the same principle here. An attack upon any human being is an attack upon the image of God and therefore an attack upon God himself. This is why God imposed the death penalty for murder way back in the beginning (Genesis 9:6). In fact, the reality of the image of God in each person should stop us from even speaking harshly to one another (James 3:9).

I hope you see where this is going. An attack upon your own life, no matter how peaceful, clinically controlled, or pain-free, is actually an attack upon the image of God and therefore an attack upon God himself. This is why it is forbidden.

"But," you may ask, "I'm going to die anyway. What difference does it make how I die? Does it really matter if I just hurry things along?"

Well, the short answer is yes, it does matter. It really does make a difference whether someone dies from cancer or from medically assisted suicide. If someone dies from a disease, they are dying from something over which they have no control. The cause of death is the fatal illness. But if someone dies from medically assisted suicide, then it is not the disease, but a fatal human act that causes that person's death. In the one case, God exercises his sovereign control over life and death. In the other case, man usurps God's authority and steals it for himself.

Some Important Distinctions
There is a real and important difference between terminating *life* and terminating ***treatment***.

I am convinced that purposely taking your own life is an affront to God. That being said, it is wrong to conclude that prolonging life is always a good thing and shortening life is always wrong. There is no biblical command, of which I am aware, that demands we submit to one more operation or one more (or any) treatment. It is completely legitimate to refuse further treatment if that treatment promises no real relief and would only extend one's misery and suffering.

Respect for life demands that even if we refuse treatment, we still must be fed and cared for. This being said, refusing treatment can mean refusing the insertion of a feeding tube. Likewise, a "do not resuscitate" order does not constitute any form of suicide. This is not actively ending a life, but merely allowing the disease to take its course.

In the same way, the removal of devices that artificially extend our lives does not constitute suicide (or murder, for that matter). All forms of suicide have one thing in common: they try to interrupt the natural processes of the body to bring about death. But the removal of artificial means of support (feeding tubes, breathing machines, and the like) do not interrupt the natural processes of the body. Such an action merely allows the natural state of the body to continue in its course.

That being said, we must quickly add that the use of such artificial life-extending treatments is not a sin either. There is no commandment of which I am aware that forbids any form of medical treatment. Medical treatment, by its very nature, is designed to interrupt the normal flow of bodily functions and enhance and/or preserve life. Therefore, if we were to forbid one type of treatment, it appears to me that we would have to forbid all forms of medication just to be consistent. Clearly we can't go that far, as the Bible records the prophet Isaiah (2 Kings 20:7) and the apostle Paul (1 Timothy 5:23) commanding the use of medicine.

We must also recognize that sometimes, especially near the end of life, loved ones are faced with the decision of administering more pain relief even when it is relatively certain that such treatment will hasten death. The important consideration in such a decision is the motivation for administering the drugs. If the motivation is to ease the patient's suffering, then this is a legitimate form of treatment. This is not the same as administering drugs for the purpose of ending the life. In such a case one has made a choice to prioritize pain relief over longevity. I am convinced that such a treatment decision does not violate the Sixth Commandment.

One other scenario must be discussed before we leave this general topic. What happens when you are no longer able to make these decisions for yourself? The obvious answer is that someone else must make them for you. But who?

One possible answer is the medical establishment providing your treatment, whether in your home or at a hospital. Because there are so many legal issues involved, most doctors and hospitals press you to create an advance directive explicitly stating your wishes, which they can keep on file.

Another possible answer is a medical power of attorney. When you are no longer able to make medical decisions for yourself, this document transfers control of those choices to another person whom you trust. This person may be your spouse, one of your children, a sibling, or even a close friend. What's important is that you trust this person to look out for your interests as you've expressed them.

For what it's worth, my wife and I have elected not to file an advance directive and rely solely on the medical power of attorney that I've given to her. Our reasoning in this decision is quite simple. As we discussed the possible scenarios that might occur, we realized that no single answer fit our wishes for every scenario. There are simply too many variables. So, I asked her to be my advocate when I was no longer able to speak for myself. I trust her judgment. We had the appropriate papers drawn up and we've placed them on file with my doctors and the local hospital. We also have a copy at home with our other important papers.

Just because my wife and I chose this route doesn't mean that you should. Your situation might be totally different from mine. That being said, I strongly suggest that you choose *something*. Make some preparations for when you can no longer speak for yourself—because the last thing you want to do is leave the important decisions of life and death in the hands of faceless bureaucrats and lawyers. Simple prudence requires that you make preparations now, if you haven't done so already.

Some Final Thoughts

It is impossible to discuss every scenario that one may face when it comes to decisions about life and death. What this chapter has attempted to do was to provide you with some general principles in order to help with those decisions.

We have seen that assisted suicide is a violation of the Sixth Commandment and an attack upon the image of God, which is in fact an attack upon God himself. That being said, we have also seen that prolonging life is not always required. Refusing treatment or prioritizing pain relief is not a violation of the Sixth Commandment. These general principles, along with a generous helping of prayer, should assist the patient and the family to make decisions in this area that they will be glad they've made when they stand before God.

Linger and Consider ...

Please give yourself time to think carefully about these questions. You will be facing decisions that you never expected you'd have to face, and you want to be prepared to approach them from a biblical standpoint. This might be a good time to talk through your answers to these questions with your spouse or a trusted friend.

Have you considered medically assisted suicide as a means of ending your suffering? Have you thought about it in light of God's command to do no murder?

Have any of your family or friends broached the subject of medically assisted suicide? Did the subject of the Sixth Commandment ever come up?

Have you made decisions concerning the limitations of your care? Are these written down someplace that is easily accessible and known to your family? Have you filed these papers with your doctors and local hospital? Have you discussed these matters with the person who has your medical power of attorney? Is that person in agreement with you? If this chapter has altered your wishes regarding any of the desires you've previously expressed, please make sure to record those changes, and make them known.

13

What Should I Be Doing Now?

One aspect of terminal illness that often goes unrecognized (at least by outsiders) is the constant loss it entails. Nearly everyone recognizes the big loss at the end of the struggle — but it is those other losses, the "little" ones that come before, that often go unnoticed by those not in the immediate family.

The problem is, these "little" losses really aren't so little, now, are they? Oh, I suppose, the early losses could be considered "little" in the vast scheme of things. Your daily run or weekly basketball game aren't absolutely necessary to life. But it hurts when you sell your motorcycle or the second car because you can't use them anymore. The sense of loss is real when you watch others do the yard work or cook the meals or babysit the grandchildren. When you're forced to quit your job, your sense of worth can take a beating. When you can no longer go fishing, or out to eat, or go out to other people's homes, it's only natural to wonder where joy and purpose may be found in life.

Some terminally ill patients take the easy way out and just withdraw. They shut down. They quit trying. They retreat into a world of passivity. Like water, they follow the path of least resistance. When their loved ones plead with them to come back, to re-engage, to live life until the end, they become surly and bad-tempered, growling, "Why can't you just leave me alone?" as they stare vacantly at the TV. Oh, I hope that doesn't describe you! I desperately hope that doesn't describe you, because God doesn't want you to live in such a miserable condition.

Our Terminally Ill Example

Now Elisha had been suffering from the illness from which he died. Jehoash king of Israel went down to see him and wept over him. "My father! My father!" he cried. "The chariots and horsemen of Israel!"

Elisha said, "Get a bow and some arrows," and he did so. "Take the bow in your hands," he said to the king of Israel. When he had taken it, Elisha put his hands on the king's hands.

"Open the east window," he said, and he opened it. "Shoot!" Elisha said, and he shot. "The LORD's arrow of victory, the arrow of victory over Aram!" Elisha declared. "You will completely destroy the Arameans at Aphek."

Then he said, "Take the arrows," and the king took them. Elisha told him, "Strike the ground." He struck it three times and stopped. The man of God was angry with him and said, "You should have struck the ground five or six times; then you would have defeated Aram and completely destroyed it. But now you will defeat it only three times."

Elisha died and was buried. (2 Kings 13:14–20a)

In this story, God has provided us an interesting example of what it means to be terminally ill, yet still active in his service. The story begins with the prophet Elisha on his deathbed. He is suffering from the illness from which he died. Put another way, he is terminally ill. When the king of Israel comes to see him, Elisha speaks the words of God to him. These words, interestingly, are words of both comfort and rebuke. Then, when this was completed, we read that Elisha died and was buried.

Now, I realize that Elisha was a special man. He was one of the most prolific miracle-workers in the Old Testament. He was able to foretell the future with exacting precision. So, in this aspect at least, we will never be like him. That being said, he still serves as an example for all who claim the title *"servant of God"*—and may I quickly add that, if you have trusted Jesus Christ as your Savior through his shed blood on the cross, this is a title that applies to you as well.

So, what can we learn from the terminally ill Elisha that might be applied to our terminally ill lives?

First, Elisha provides an example of determination and effort to the very end of his life. Elisha is more than 80 years old when the events of this story happen. Yet, despite his age, and even though he is stricken with a deadly disease, he never loses interest in the affairs of this life. He doesn't give himself up to inaction. He doesn't withdraw. Instead, he engages the weeping king of Israel for the king's own good and the good of the country.

Second, he doesn't use his illness as an excuse. In the scene described here, Elisha tells the king to take a bow and some arrows and to assume the stance of an archer (*"take the bow in your hands"*). Then, in an act that probably took all of his physical strength, Elisha rises from his sickbed, stands either next to or behind the king, and places his hands on the king's hands, so it looks like both of them are shooting the arrow together. Put another way, he actively participates in this symbolic drama. Even though Elisha, at his age and in his condition, might've been excused for merely taking the king's visit as the compliment it was intended to be and remaining in his sickbed, he uses all the strength he has available until the very end.

Third, Elisha evidently saw every encounter as a ministry opportunity. You may not remember a lot about Elisha, so let me fill in a little background.

Unlike his mentor, Elijah, Elisha didn't spend a lot of time in the spotlight. He isn't remembered for one great encounter, like Elijah at Mount Carmel. Instead, Elisha could be found, more often than not, with ordinary people. He performed his miracles — and he performed a lot of miracles — away from the crowds, beyond the view of the television cameras. By all appearances, it seems that he was never content unless he used every encounter as an opportunity to minister.

And so it is here. Even on his deathbed, Elisha rouses the king from his despair and gives him hope, courage, and energy. He encourages the king to have faith in the LORD, and then rebukes him when he responds halfheartedly. Put another way, Elisha still had a message to give, a message that he wouldn't have been able to communicate effectively if he had lost all hope himself.

There is much we can learn from Elisha. We may learn that, while we still live, we still have opportunities for ministry. Even on our deathbeds, we may still be agents for good. We may advise, exhort, encourage, and, yes, even rebuke evil. In fact, we may do so as we've never done before, because when we speak in the midst of a terminal illness, our words have a greater impression than when everything is normal and fine.

The Purpose of Life

At times like these, it's good to be reminded that the purpose of your life is the same as it has always been. In other words, your terminal diagnosis has not changed what God desires of you. For example, *"He has shown you, O mortal, what is good. And what does the LORD require of you? To act justly and to love mercy and to walk humbly with your God"* (Micah 6:8). There is no "unless you're terminally ill, then you don't have to" clause in this command. This command is given to all people at all times and in all circumstances. That being said, we must admit that figuring out how to do this in concrete and explicit terms is somewhat difficult when you're confined to bed.

That's why I think the apostle Paul's command is more immediately helpful to those of us who are terminally ill. He writes, *"So whether you eat or drink or whatever you do, do it all for the glory of God"* (1 Corinthians 10:31). I see this as more helpful because the apostle Paul makes it clear that as long as you are living, you are to do whatever it is you still can do, no matter how limited, to the glory of God.

But what does this mean in practice? What does living to the glory of God actually look like? To answer this question, we must first answer a more basic question: what do we mean by "glory of God?"

Understanding the Glory of God

Disclaimer: When writing about a theological concept, the temptation (at least for me) is to become overly technical. The more precise one is in defining something, the less likely one is to slip into error. The downside to that approach is that exacting precision is almost always the enemy of clarity, and clarity is, above all else, what I'm striving for here. I've written on the subject of the "glory of God" elsewhere with as much precision as I can muster. If you're interested in a (much) deeper dive into the subject, I encourage you to look there.[17] This treatment, in contrast, though not quite as precise, is designed to communicate the basic truths I've written about earlier, while being as accessible as possible.

Virtually all theologians would agree, at least at some level, that the glory of God involves a demonstration or presentation of who God is as a person. When we glorify God, we put on display what God is like. Why does God require us to *"act justly and love mercy?"* Because God always acts justly and always loves mercy, that's why. We are called to glorify God in all that we do, and one means of doing so is to act as much like God as possible.

Now, of course, we have to realize that all our attempts to act like God fall pitifully short of what God is actually like. For you see, God is without limits. There are no boundaries that can be placed on any aspect of God's being. This means that when he loves, there is no limit to his love. Likewise, there is no limit to his compassion or mercy or grace. The same cannot be said of us. In the same way, although we may be truthful in our speech and actions, we can never be truthful as God is truthful simply because we have limits and he does not.

So, what does this mean in practice? One way we glorify God is when we act as much like God as possible. When we do what he would do, say what he would say, think what he would think, have the same emotions that he would have, we glorify God. In the same way, whenever we refuse to say what God wouldn't say or refuse to do what God wouldn't do or refuse to think what God wouldn't think or refuse to have an emotion that God wouldn't have, we glorify God. The more we act like God, the more we obey the apostle Paul and glorify God in all that we do.

We must understand that, while it is possible for us to reproduce some aspects of God's character in our own lives, it is impossible for us to mirror all aspects of God's perfections in what we do. A moment's consideration shows this to be obvious. God is all-powerful, for example. This means he can bring into existence any reality that he desires. Clearly, we are unable to do that. After all, if we were all-powerful, then we wouldn't still be sick, now would we? In the same way, God knows all things. Not only does he know all those things that have been, are, or will be, but he also knows all the infinite possibilities of all those things that might have been or could be. He knows all these things without having to investigate or learn. How unlike God we are in this respect! We could continue this line of thought by discussing how God is everywhere at once, filling all space and time, or about how God is ageless and eternal, but I think you see the point.

The obvious question at this point then becomes, "Is it possible to glorify God even in those aspects of his being that I cannot reproduce?" The answer is, surprisingly, yes. Let me show you how.

According to David, we glorify God when we thank him and praise him for what he has done on our behalf (Psalms 86:12–13). This makes perfect sense. Although we may not do the things that God has done, we may still put those actions and attributes on display by declaring them with our lips and in our prayers.

In fact, the apostle Paul prays that we might have endurance and encouragement so that the church as a whole might, with one mind and with one voice, glorify God together (Romans 15:5–6).

I find it interesting that Paul considers endurance a prerequisite to our glorifying God: By making endurance a necessary condition to our glorifying God, Paul is recognizing something basic about our human condition. First, he is acknowledging that everyone has trouble. Oh, some have more trouble than others, to be sure, but everyone has some burden weighing them down. But what is true of everyone generally is especially true of those with a terminal illness. Therefore, we should be praying to God that he would give us endurance so that we might continue to praise him and give him glory even in the most difficult of life's circumstances.

We may also glorify God by the way that we die. Jesus told Peter that he would be crucified and so indicated to Peter *"the kind of death by which Peter would glorify God"* (John 21:17). Now, we must be sure to understand what this does — and does not — mean. This does not mean that death, by itself, glorifies God. Death is always portrayed as an enemy in the Bible. Likewise, even though death comes to all people, not all people glorify God in their death. What this does mean, however, is that the way that we die may glorify God. Exhibiting the peace that only God can give when it's our turn to die glorifies God. Maintaining a faithful testimony to the very end glorifies God. Encouraging our loved ones to always trust in him as the time draws near glorifies God. I don't know about you, but I've been praying that I will die well — that in my death, God would be glorified, so that my suffering and death would not merely be a wasted opportunity, but rather that his name would be lifted up and glorified.

Living every moment to the glory of God is at once a command and a privilege. But it isn't easy. I know this is a tall order. Believe me, I know! At the very best of times our obedience to this command will be partial and limited. But even our feeble attempts, as clumsy and as failing as they are, are pleasing in God's sight.

The best analogy I know to explain this is of a toddler learning to walk. No parent is ever satisfied until their child is able to run and jump with grace and skill. Nevertheless, when that first step or two is taken, no matter how awkward and ungainly the child is, Mom and Dad swell with pride.

They take pictures and call the grandparents to inform them of how above average their grandchild is! Beloved, our Heavenly Father is no different. He isn't satisfied until we are able to be exactly as he is in his character. Nevertheless, he is delighted with our first wobbly steps.

This being said, even when we fail him, we may still glorify him. According to Revelation 16:9, our repentance also glorifies him. So even when we fail — and don't kid yourself, we will fail — our quick repentance restores us to fellowship and glorifies God.

Linger and Consider ...

This chapter provides an opportunity for some very hard work, as you seek to bring your attitudes and actions into submission to your beliefs. This is a "where the rubber meets the road" chapter. Stop, and let's think it through together.

Now that you know all this, what is it in your life that should change? Or maybe this is a better question: Are you ready to work toward glorifying God in all that you do even in the midst of your suffering, even though your body is failing, with a view to dying well? Are you praying toward that end?

14

Spurgeon's Challenge

Charles Haddon Spurgeon (1834–1892) was a highly influential preacher in England during his lifetime. Even today his lectures and sermons (numbering in the thousands) are widely studied and quoted. Even though he was a Baptist, he remains a powerful figure in numerous other denominations and traditions and is still known in seminaries across the world as "The Prince of Preachers."

Before an "audience of invalid ladies," Spurgeon preached his sermon "Beloved, and Yet Afflicted"—a treatment of John 11:3 (*So the sisters sent word to Jesus, "Lord, the one you love is sick."*) The words with which he concluded this sermon are also a fitting conclusion to this book.

> If Jesus loves you, and you are sick, let all the world see how you glorify God in your sickness. Let friends and nurses see how the beloved of the Lord are cheered and comforted by him. Let your holy resignation astonish them, and set them admiring your Beloved, who is so gracious to you that he makes you happy in pain, and joyful at the gates of the grave. If your religion is worth anything it ought to support you now, and it will compel unbelievers to see that he whom the Lord loveth is in better case when he is sick than the ungodly when full of health and vigour.[18]

I began this book by stating my reason for writing. It was because people kept telling me I was different. The peace that I exhibited and my joyful attitude set me apart from others with my disease. I mentioned that this had nothing to do with me but rather with the one I knew and with what he had promised. We have examined those promises within this book. We have reviewed together how to be right with him so that we no longer fear death. Now is the time to put those truths into action.

My prayer for you, beloved, is that your life will be so totally transformed by the truths presented in this book that people will look at you the same way they look at me: As someone who possesses something different. As someone who has a peace that surpasses all comprehension.

Your challenge in the next fifteen minutes, the next week, the next month, and as long as the Lord gives you here on earth, is to show the world that the one whom the Lord loves is in a better situation when he is sick than the unbeliever is when he is healthy. It's time to show the world that because … well … it's so very, very true.

It's true because, of all the people in the world, we are the ones who do not need to fear death. *Everyone dies.* Despite that obvious fact, most people in their day-to-day lives never give that a thought. We, in contrast, are different. We have been forced to look death in the face and find out what we really believe. We, unlike most others, have been given the gift of time: time to make things right between ourselves and other people and between ourselves and God.

When you're terminally ill, the promises of God concerning the future take on a new significance. We, unlike all others, may take a realistic and joyous view about the reason for our suffering, the timing of our death, and what happens when that time comes. We alone have a future so bright that we may consider our departure from this world to be *"better by far."*

We have also been given the time to minister in a special way. As Spurgeon observed, it's a time when our "friends and nurses [may] see how the beloved of the Lord are cheered and comforted" by his promises. Our lives should be so different that it would "compel unbelievers to see that he whom the Lord loveth is in better case when he is sick than the ungodly when full of health and vigour."

The promises God has made concerning our present and our future allow us to say with David, *"I will fear no evil, for thou art with me,"*[19] which, of course, is the title of this book. It is my prayer that God will use this little book to help you say exactly that with a genuine smile and a peaceful heart.

Linger and Consider ...

I've asked you after every chapter to sit a while with the truths presented and think them through. I'm going to ask that again now. I don't close this chapter with specific questions, but rather a suggestion that you review what you've written up to now, as well as this last chapter, and do some writing about what the Lord brings to your mind and heart.

15

"Weep Not for Me"

From a funeral sermon by Matthew Henry (1662–1714)[20]

If you consider the happiness I am entered into, that fair palace in which death was but a dark entry, you would not weep for me, but rejoice rather.

Would you know where I am? I am at home in my Father's house, in the mansion prepared for me there. I am where I would be, where I have long and often desired to be; no longer on a stormy sea, but in a safe and quiet harbour. My working time is done, and I am resting: my sowing time is done, and I am reaping; my joy is as the joy of harvest.

Would you know how it is with me? I am made perfect in holiness; grace is swallowed up in glory; the top-stone of the building is brought forth.

Would you know what I am doing? I see God, I see him as he is, not as through a glass darkly, but face to face; and the sight is transforming, it makes me like him. I am in the sweet enjoyment of my blessed Redeemer, ... whom my soul loved, and for whose sake I was willing to part with all; I am here bathing myself at the spring-head of heavenly pleasures and joys unutterable, and therefore weep not for me....I am here singing Hallelujahs incessantly to him who sits upon the throne, and rest not day or night from praising him.

Would you know what company I have? Blessed company, better than the best on earth; here are holy angels and the spirits of just men made perfect; I am set down with

Abraham, and Isaac, and Jacob in the kingdom of God, with blessed Paul, and Peter, and James, and John, and all the saints; and here I meet with many of my old acquaintances, that I fasted and prayed with, who got before me hither.

And, lastly, will you consider how long this is to continue: it is a garland that never withers; a crown of glory that fades not away; after millions of millions of ages, it will be as fresh as it is now; and therefore weep not for me.

It is true, the body must turn to rottenness and putrefaction, the worms must feed sweetly upon it; but that also sleeps in Jesus, it still remains united to him, and shall shortly be raised again incorruptible, like the glorious body of Jesus Christ, more glorious than the noon-day sun.

ENDNOTES

[1] "At convention, heart doctors lean toward burgers and fries." *Boston Globe*, November 10, 1993.

[2] David P. Phillips, George C. Liu, Kennon Kwok, Jason R. Jarvinen, et al., "The *Hound of the Baskervilles* effect: natural experiment on the influence of psychological stress on timing of death." *British Medical Journal* 323 (22–29 December 2001): 1443–1446.

[3] Ibid., 1445.

[4] Neil Boyce, "… fear itself." *New Scientist–UK Edition* 161 (March 6, 1999): 35.

[5] S. H. Kellogg, *A Handbook of Comparative Religion* (Philadelphia: Westminster Press, 1899), 6–10.

[6] Ibid., 6–7.

[7] Unless otherwise stated, all Scripture citations are taken from the *New International Version*.

[8] Erik Larson, *Dead Wake: The Last Crossing of the Lusitania* (New York: Broadway Books, 2016), 254–255.

[9] ISO 14644–1:2015: Clean rooms and associated controlled environments — Part 1: Classification of air cleanliness by particle concentration (December 2015).

[10] United States v. Wilson, 32 U.S. 150, 160–61 (1833).

[11] This outline isn't original with me. I remember hearing it as a child from my pastor, Dr. Bruce W. Dunn, of Grace Presbyterian Church in Peoria, Illinois.

[12] As this outline is not original with me, neither is this illustration. I heard it long ago, although I cannot remember where.

[13] Taken from the *NIV* 1984 translation.

[14] This chapter deals with a particular area of Bible prophecy. While there are differing ideas about the exact nature and timing of these events, this chapter is centered around those truths that are self-evident from this text alone to provide the maximum comfort level intended by God.

[15] We should note that this final question is not asked only by the terminally ill. Others ask (and answer) this question for a variety of reasons. The comedian Robin Williams, for example, lost that which he felt was central to who he was: the ability to be funny. The loss of this ability, by which he defined his life, drove him to suicide. Susannah Cahalan, "How Robin Williams was being torn apart and couldn't fight back," *New York Post*, May 5, 2018. In contrast, David Goodall, the famed Australian scientist, wasn't ill. He committed (medically assisted) suicide because he was old. The 104-year-old said, "My feeling is that an old person like myself should have full citizenship rights, including the right of assisted suicide." Lindsey Bever, "David Goodall, 104, just took his own life, after making a powerful statement about assisted death," *The Washington Post*, May 10, 2018.

[16] Thomas Cahill, *The Gifts of the Jews: How a Tribe of Desert Nomads Changed the Way Everyone Thinks and Feels* (New York: Nan A. Talese/Anchor, 1998), 142.

[17] Bruce A. Baker, "A biblical and theological examination of the glory of god," *Journal of Ministry & Theology* 22, no. 1 (Spring 2018): 5–25.

[18] C. H. Spurgeon, "Beloved, and Yet Afflicted," in *The Metropolitan Tabernacle Pulpit Sermons* vol. 26 (London: Passmore & Alabaster, 1880); 76 in Logos Bible Software.

[19] Psalm 23:4, *KJV*.

[20] Matthew Henry, "A Concise Account of the Life of Mr Samuel Lawrence," in *The Complete Works of Matthew Henry: Treatises, Sermons, and Tracts*, vol. 2 (Baker Publishing Group, Kindle Edition), Kindle Location 31395–31397.

Another book by Bruce Baker

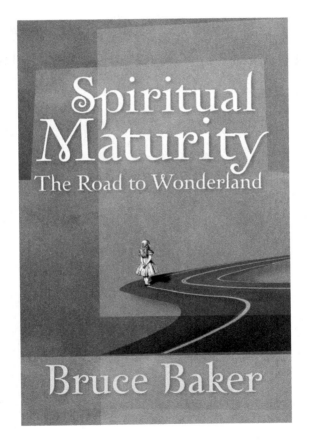

Available at GraceAcresPress.com
or wherever books are sold.

Growing Your Faith One Page at a Time

Resources for Cultivating Joy
Small Group—Sunday School—Personal Study

Grace Acres Press
GraceAcresPress.com
303-681-9995

CPSIA information can be obtained
at www.ICGtesting.com
Printed in the USA
FSHW011728030619
58679FS